Power and Parliament

Power and Parliament

TIMOTHY RAISON

BASIL BLACKWELL · OXFORD

To Kate and Paul

by request!

British Library Cataloguing in Publication Data

Raison, Timothy
  Power Parliament
  1. Great Britain—Politics and Government—1964
  2. Power (Social Sciences)
  I. Title
  320.9,41,0857   JN231

  ISBN 0 631 11301 0

Typeset by Cotswold Typesetting Ltd., Gloucester and
Printed in Great Britain by
Billing and Sons Ltd.
London, Guildford and Worcester

Contents

Acknowledgements

Like all books of this kind, *Power and Parliament* owes much of any merit that it may have to the author's discussions and arguments with friends and colleagues over a period of years. I am particularly in debt to the One Nation Group of Tory MPs for their comments on my proposals on the House of Lords (although the group did not all agree with me). Another debt is to the Centre of Studies for Social Policy (now merged into the Policy Studies Institute), where I spent three and a half rewarding years as a part-time Senior Fellow, and edited a symposium on the corporate state, contributing a paper on which I draw heavily in chapter 3.

I would like to acknowledge specific debts to *The Times* for permission to reproduce the extract from David Wood's article 'Either way we vote to Downgrade Parliament', and to Messrs Hutchinson for permission to quote an extract from Sir Ian Gilmour's important *Inside Right*. I owe thanks as well to the editors of *The Daily Telegraph*, *The Spectator* and *The Planner* for permission to use passages from articles of my own that originally appeared in their columns.

I would like to thank the Mainstream board for their helpful comments on my book, and Annabel Linney and Barbara Wallis for their valiant typing of the manuscript.

1

Introduction

With hindsight, it may seem that the decades between 1918, when British women first received the suffrage, and the early 1970s represented an unusual lull in the process of constitutional change—a lull exceeded in length only by the period which followed the Glorious Revolution. Both before and after the 1939 war, the constitution seemed remarkably settled. There was plenty to worry about; but the worry was in terms of what governments should do and what resources they had rather than whether they had the political strength and authority to do it. Of course there were constitutional changes—the Parliament Act of 1949, for example, the introduction of life peerages and later the extension of the suffrage to eighteen-year-olds; but these caused relatively little excitement. There was also, during the 1960s in particular, growing dissatisfaction with the detailed workings of Parliament and the executive and with the structure of local government and the health service, and indeed with many other institutions. But again the basic assumptions about our constitution and where political power should lie in our society were not widely challenged.

My book *Why Conservative?* (Penguin, 1964) paid no regard to the questions about the locus and legitimacy of power in our society that have agitated us since the mid-1970s. They simply were not burning issues at that time. What are the challenges and anxieties which have so altered the scene?

Undoubtedly the most traumatic (particularly, though far from exclusively, for Conservatives) has been the growing strength of trade unions. I will not analyse here the troubled sequence of events between the Wilson government's attempt to reform the trade unions at the end of the 1960s and the confrontation between the Heath government and the miners in 1973–74; but the slogan of 1974—'Who governs?'—and the outcome of that dispute sum up the essence of that challenge. By then it seemed to many people that for the first time unions had effectively used their latent 'giant's strength' in a political framework and that government had been exposed as unable to resist the challenge.

In 1952, the National Council of Labour, representing the TUC, the Labour Party and the Cooperative Union made this statement: 'The National Council of Labour expresses in strongest terms its condemnation of the attempts now being made by irresponsible elements to persuade trade unionists to take industrial action to achieve political ends. Such action, in addition to threatening the economy of the nation, is in itself a direct challenge to the supremacy of our established democratic institutions' (*The Times*, 27 February 1952). We did not often hear words like that under the Heath government.

There are different views as to why unions have seemed more ready to make use of their powers. Some attribute the change to new factors such as the availability of supplementary benefits to strikers and their families as well as to tax rebates. Some say that the centralization or interdependence of public services, such as electricity, brought about by new technology, has made society more vulnerable. Some see it more in terms of attitudes. Some argue that the new militancy has been provoked by misguided policies, for example over incomes. Some ascribe it to the influence of communists and Trotskyists. But whatever the reasons, the resistance by the Upper Clyde Shipbuilders' workers, the retreat by the police before mass picketing at Saltley, the affair of the imprisoned five dockers and their release, and the 1973–74 miners' strike rightly or wrongly left many people feeling that a new element has entered the political scene.

Another development can be described as a drift towards corporatism. It took different forms: the suggestion that NEDC should be elevated to provide a national bargaining forum and the tripartite talks instigated by Mr Heath; the Social Contract of Sir Harold Wilson and Mr Callaghan; and occasional proposals for an industrial parliament. Each implies a power-sharing relationship between Government and industry (or anyway the unions) and therefore seemed to give a new constitutional status to bodies which in the past had simply been the major pressure groups.

The growth of union power was only one sign of change in our familiar conventions. The same period has seen the growth of violent demonstrations (including militant picketing); the resurgence of terrorism, notably in Northern Ireland; and a generally wider willingness to take arguments away from Parliament and to convert them into struggle in the streets. But apart from violence and demonstrations, lawful or otherwise, there has been a greater tendency to challenge the very authority or legitimacy of Parliamentary and local authority decision-taking as we have known them.

The issue is partly about consent. Some argue that it is not enough to elect representatives and then empower them to carry on making the necessary decisions until the next election: they must always govern with the recurrent consent of the people—not so much as the people as a whole, as the people concerned in particular issues. Thus the legitimacy of the Industrial Relations Act of 1971 was questioned because it did not carry the consent of the union movement; the legitimacy of the Housing Finance Act of 1972 was challenged because it was said not to have the consent of local authorities or council tenants; and so on.

Local government has seen this issue raised mainly in terms of the right of participation in decision-making, a right which embraces, but may go beyond, the right to be consulted. Admittedly, not many people would argue that the duty of local authorities (or the Secretary of State) to decide a planning matter should be formally handed over to a majority of the participants in an enquiry or to those who get most signatures on a petition. Nevertheless, there is an increasing assumption that the expressed views of participants should be decisive, and increasing disappointment when such views are not accepted. All this, in turn, arguably makes it harder for government to get on with the business of governing.

An even more fundamental challenge to our tradition of Parliamentary and local government decision-making comes from socialists or syndicalists who place either party or worker groups above Parliament. The socialists tend to see the crucial democratic decision to be the vote of the party conference as

subsequently expressed in a manifesto. The point was illustrated by Mr Eric Heffer in the Second Reading Debate on the
Scotland Bill (14 November 1977) when he said that he thought
that the Government were 'totally wrong' about the Scotland
Bill, but that because the Bill appeared in the Labour Manifesto
he would 'sustain the Government while urging them to change
their minds'. He also said 'I have always argued in this House in
favour of the Manifesto'. This comes from a left-winger who is
also a good parliamentarian; others on the left tip the balance
further towards the party.

The notion that democracy lies with the party decision conflicts with the traditional assumption that the only true democratic expression of view derives from the votes of *all* the people
(rather than a group of party members); and which holds that it
is the duty of Members of Parliament to exercise their own
judgement in the interests of the nation, rather than be bound
by manifesto, mandates or the decisions of extra-parliamentary
bodies. The mere fact that a party has come to a decision by a
vote open to all its members has not made that a 'democratic'
decision. The traditional view is that democracy is to do with
people as a whole rather than with particular organizations or
interest groups. The sovereignty of the party has been seen as a
characteristic of East European socialism, not of liberal democracy. The Left of today, however, think differently.

One particular argument for party control is that the practice
of electing MPs and councillors and then leaving them to run
things until the next election enables them to operate without
effective advice, scrutiny and criticism (not that it feels like this
to ministers!). The job of the party is seen as making sure that
ministers and councillors are kept continuously on their toes,
acting in accordance with party policy. Constitutional conservatives would say that this scrutiny is primarily the job of Parliament, though rank-and-file Conservatives in the country are
often heard to demand that their voice should be more closely
heeded by their leaders.

The other notion favoured by the Left, that power or legitimacy should lie with particular worker groups, is equally alien
to our tradition. It has not taken very strong hold in Britain, to
date at least. Though Mr Tony Benn seems to lend a sympathetic
ear to advocates of workers' control, the trade union movement

has not generally shown much interest in it, and so far as its leadership is concerned still tends to be centralist in its instincts. Indeed, it is ambivalent about the question of worker participation in management raised in the Bullock Report. Nevertheless, there are those who favour forms of localized workers' control through co-operatives, not least because they represent a way of meeting the bureaucratization that is one of the endemic characteristics of socialism.

So far, I have dealt mainly with challenges to our traditional parliamentary system from what may be loosely called the Left. But there are two major developments that are not necessarily associated with the Left: the thesis that Parliament (or anyway the Commons), far from being too weak, is in fact too strong, and may constitute what has been described by Lord Hailsham as an 'elective dictatorship'; and the introduction into our political system of a direct appeal to the people through referenda. The essence of the first case is that a party that is able to command a bare majority in the Commons, and which has the votes of only a comparatively small minority of the electorate as a whole in its favour, may nevertheless do much as it likes in Parliament, passing legislation to which the House of Lords can only offer strictly limited resistance. The implication is that all existing laws can be up-ended by such a minority government, that there is no Bill of Rights or written constitution to act as a check, and that the Common Law is easily overcome by fresh statutes. Many who take this view look not only to a Bill of Rights and/or a written constitution, a stronger Second Chamber and perhaps a more active judiciary to offset the present power of the Commons, but also to proportional representation as a restraint on the runaway actions of a minority party.

Proportional representation and reform of the Lords, as I write, are still only in the realms of argument, though PR has been used in Northern Ireland; but the referendum has become a fact. It was used by the last Conservative government to determine the allegiance of Northern Ireland; it was used by the Labour government to resolve the question of British membership of the EEC; and it was brought into the devolution legislation to give the people of Scotland and Wales a decisive voice in whether the Bills should be implemented. It was also espoused by Mrs Thatcher in September 1977 as a means of dealing with challenges to government, notably from unions.

In some ways, the referendum represents as dramatic a switch in the locus of power in our society as any. The UK Parliament as a whole relinquishes, either to the people as a whole or particular groups of them, the right to decide certain major matters. This raises great questions: when a referendum should be used; how to make sure that it is 'fair' in its timing, presentation and wording; whether an appeal to the people will bring populism at its worst; whether people will always understand the issues on which they vote; whether it may be a tool for potential dictators of anyway over-mighty individuals. But above all, perhaps, it raises the question of whether handing some decisions directly to the people will not undermine confidence in the legitimacy of Parliament when it takes decisions in those matters which remain with it.

But the referendum is not the only major change in the location of power that is already under way. Devolution, if it happens, is clearly another. So perhaps, though less obviously, is the erosion of the independence of local government as it increasingly becomes an agent for central government policy. Above all, of course, membership of the EEC has implications which cannot yet be described or even discerned, but which must be of great significance, though I shall not examine them in this book.

The constitutional field is thus more active than it has been for years. This is indisputable. This book is an attempt to explore these stirrings and to point to the directions which we might take in responding to them. It is about where power lies in our society, and how power functions; it is also about where power ought to lie and how it ought to function. It is a political book, written by an avowed Tory; and it is concerned with decisions that come within the public domain, whether nationally or locally. Essentially, it asks whether our traditional forms of liberal democracy within a pluralist society and of the rule of law are still valid.

Perhaps at this point a detailed critical analysis of what that kind of society means should be undertaken; but to do that would be to embark on a new Dicey or a new Bagehot, and that is not my purpose. Yet a rough and ready summary of some of the ingredients in the system or pattern which is now under challenge from these various quarters is necessary.

First, there is the sovereignty of the Crown in Parliament, which means for most purposes the House of Commons. Its legitimacy is derived both from history and now from universal adult suffrage. It provides the executive, which in general exercises powers conferred on it by statute together with the power to take actions which are not prohibited by statute. In certain fields—notably foreign affairs—it operates under the royal prerogative (that is, without statutory sanction), though ministers are in effect accountable to Parliament in these matters. O Hood Phillips, in *Constitutional and Administrative Law* (Sweet and Maxwell, 4th Edition, 1967), says that 'A Government shall not advise the Crown to declare war, make peace or conclude a treaty unless there is ample ground for supposing that the majority of the Commons approves the policy'. I am not sure that this need always be so; but what is clear that a government that takes action of this kind can always subsequently be forced by the Commons to resign. Treaties anyway often entail consequential legislation.

Coupled with the sovereignty of Parliament is the principle of accountability: the idea that public and publicly funded activities should ultimately be subject to some sort of elected political control. The Crown and the Courts occupy a special position in this respect; but otherwise the public sector (in its loosest definition) normally operates subject to the constraints that its funds can be withdrawn and its heads dismissed if government and Parliament (or local government) are so minded. Sometimes this control is exercised very much at second hand or within limitations, as with the BBC, the University Grants Commission, the Arts Council or the Research Councils, and perhaps the water authorities, or at the local government level by school governors if the report of the Taylor committee on that subject were implemented. But by and large, the notion of accountability still prevails.

Next, there is the principle of the rule of law. This implies that all must operate under the law and that the judiciary should be independent (even though appointed by a member of the government and in certain circumstances dismissable by Parliament). There are, of course, arguments about when one may resist an unjust law (a law sanctioning genocide, for example);

but in contemporary terms a more pressing issue may be the relationship between the judiciary and the executive and the question of judicial review of legislative acts. This has come to a head recently both through Lord Scarman's famous lectures on 'English Law—the New Dimension' and through the willingness of the Court of Appeals to restrain the power of Secretaries of State in matters like Tameside and the Laker Skytrain.

There is also a historical convention, which again has come under challenge recently, that all should be equal before the law and that it is the duty of government to be as even-handed as possible. The nature of this principle is best illustrated by describing the challenges to it. Believers in collective and social justice argue that laws must be tipped in favour of disadvantaged groups—trade unions, coloured people or women, for example. There is the growth of the notion of positive discrimination or affirmative action—the first essentially to do with allocating extra resources to hard-pressed groups, the latter with the idea that it is proper for certain groups of individuals to be given preferential access to publicly provided benefits like university education or local authority jobs. There is also an increasing readiness among governments not just to distribute economic help to areas or industries on a general basis but to pick and choose between different private companies in allocating financial help —whether on the grounds that they are worth backing or simply to keep jobs alive. This is a modern form of arbitrary government, and even if it is sanctified by law, it could undermine the principle of even-handedness, which is tied up with another principle under pressure—that so far as is possible there should be a distinction between the public and the private sphere. In the former, obviously government is the master. In the latter, government's role was seen as no more than regulatory (and taxatious—if I may coin a word!). The reverse of this traditional principle is corporatism.

Alongside even-handedness is the principle that political parties should be independent entities, not organs of the state. Of course they are intimately bound up with the state, providing as they do both the government and the official opposition; but they must not be manipulated by government in a way that could destroy their independence. If the parties were to become financial creatures of the state we could again be on the way to corporatism—or outright totalitarianism. Just as much as unions, businessmen, professions, artists or anyone else, the parties are elements in a pluralist society, even though their parliamentary members have a special role in helping to make the laws which ultimately control that society.

So much, then, for the established principles which underlie our system. This book asks whether the challenges to these principles and traditions are causing a breakdown in the system, and whether these challenges deserve to succeed or fail. Is the elaborate control mechanism which governs our country due for replacement?

Of course it will be said that the concerns which I have described represent nothing new. I myself was struck by stumbling upon a passage in a book by Herman Finer published by the Fabian Society in 1923 (*Representative Government and a Parliament of Industry*), talking of the pre-1914 period:

> All the panaceas offered just before the war—reform of the House of Commons' procedure, devolution, reform of the Second Chamber, Proportional Representation, the resuscitation of the Royal Veto, the Referendum, Round Table conferences—spoke the same language: before vital problems the old machine of party government, upon which Parliamentary and Cabinet government rest, inaugurated by the introduction of practically universal suffrage, was breaking down.

The system went on with little change: somehow those ideas were washed away by the tide of the 1914–18 war. Things have moved on, however; of the panaceas only the Royal Veto is not (so far) once again on our agenda today.

2

What Sort of Freedom?

This book is about the locus of power; but its premise is that power must not be enemy of freedom. Freedom is far and away our most valuable political heirloom: even the creation of the nation state as the means of protecting our people and promoting their interests comes second to it. Of course this latter has meant imposing many restraints on the freedom of individuals— some necessary, some not. But at the end of the day the true justification for the nation state is that it helps people to be free —to work as they wish, to say what they wish, to come and go as they wish, to have their own possessions, to be safe, to believe and worship what they wish, to live a family life, to be free from slavery and arbitrary incarceration, to be ruled under the law rather than be executive fiat, and so on. These are not absolutely untrammelled freedoms. As one writes them down, one can see that limits in fact apply to most of them—and some of these limits (such as those intended to check the unbridled production of pornography or to prevent terrorism) are backed by compelling reasons. Nevertheless, an ever more free society should be the supreme political goal and the fundamental justification for western democracy.

But there is always dispute about the nature of freedom. Traditionally, freedom has been envisaged in terms of freedom for the individual. The freedoms which I have just listed are essentially rights for individuals and protections against arbitrary demands and impositions, by the state in particular. They have been embodied in our history in all sorts of ways— for example Magna Carta and Bills of Rights. Equally important, the idea of individual freedom was expressed in the judgements and traditions of the Common Law, in the notion of equity. (It is this 'bias' in favour of the individual which has caused trade unionists to say that the judges are prejudiced against them, and consternation among cricket administrators in the Packer case). And statute law, too, sometimes explicitly protects the interests of individuals—as consumers, as appellants against executive decisions (though all too often through tribunal machinery rather than the courts), and those adversely effected by planning decisions.

Individual freedom has also been expressed in our economic philosophy. The notion of *laisser faire* and its modern modified form, the social market economy (with its acceptance of social services), has allowed people to express themselves and improve their lives through their economic actions; and it has been backed by the right to own property (strongly based in the Common Law) and to exercise considerable freedom in its use and disposition. Of course, this freedom over property has been very much curtailed, for example, by tax and planning laws. But at least a right to property still persists. The right to pass some of it on to the next generation has not been extinguished. We have not yet reached the stage where it is assumed that everything belongs to the state, which may or may not then grant bits of it to its citizens to hold by the state's permission. Taxes still have to be approved by vote and by and large we still observe the fundamental tradition that governments should breach neither the law nor the spirit of the law. We can still identify arm twisting, like the withholding of government work from firms which have broken the non-statutory incomes limits, as the exception (if an increasingly frequent exception). And though government may take any action so long as there is no legal bar to it, so long as it does not impose legally binding burdens or risks and so long as the necessary supply has been voted, we are not yet a totalitarian society.

Yet there are real challenges to individual freedom. They come mostly in the name of collective or social justice; and their justification by and large lies in the defence of the underdog and the search for equality. There is also a belief that the goals desired by the majority of the population can only be achieved by collective action through state intervention.

The search for collective or social justice has taken a variety of forms. We can see it most clearly in the field of industrial relations. The most obvious contemporary example of the clash between the collective and the individual is the closed shop. The closed shop is clearly a restraint of trade, a limitation on a worker's freedom to work where he wishes; yet it is held to be a necessary means of improving the circumstances of a group of workers as a whole. Another, perhaps more fundamental, example of social justice is acceptance (confirmed by the Donovan Commission on industrial relations) of the fact that bargains between management and unions should not have the binding force of the normal contract: custom overrides what might be thought of as the normal legal process. Recent legislation on health and safety at work and on pensions and the proposals of the Bullock Committee on 'industrial democracy' all illustrate this collective approach: they stipulate that workers must be represented by trade unions, rather than whomever they choose. It may also be argued that pickets have in practice a freedom to pursue actions which would not be permitted to other citizens. (Could street salesmen, for example, use the methods of peaceful persuasion permitted to pickets?) Again this is a form of collective freedom.

Another controversial example of legislation based on the notion of collective or social justice is to be found in anti-discrimination legislation dealing with race and sex. Free speech may be limited by it; the right to employ whom you wish is certainly limited; so is the right, for example, of a school or college to decide what proportion of its students should be male and female, once some mixed element has been admitted.

A related development, as I have already said, is what is known in Britain as positive discrimination and in the United States as affirmative action. These practices imply that in order to produce an ultimate equality preferential treatment should be given to disadvantaged groups—as in the Plowden notion of Educational Priority Areas or the allocation of substantial funds to inner cities. Or it may go further, as it has done in the United States, with widespread bussing of school children in order to secure a more equal racial and cultural mix, and the reservation of a number of places at educational or other public institutions for members of disadvantaged minority groups, so that those with inferior qualifications from these groups may nevertheless gain places at the expense of others with superior qualifications. Something of the same sort may be seen in a mild way in

Oxbridge colleges which feel they should tip the balance in favour of those who come from comprehensive schools; but their concern here is to seek out latent ability, rather than tip the balance as a whole in favour of a particular group.

These developments may be seen as part of a movement away from the notion of even-handed government which has been by and large a part of our tradition. This notion implies that government should not pick and choose among citizens: it should act on rules which are applicable to all. It has always been a difficult principle to operate, not least because governments dispose of enormous amounts of contracts and patronage. At least rules about competitive tendering, and the scrutiny of the Public Accounts Committee and the audit system, provide some sort of safeguard over contracts. But in recent years the introduction of industrial support has made the system more and more arbitrary: the law of the land now allows one firm but not another to receive a subsidy, in effect at the whim of government. Under the Callaghan government's stage three incomes policy, some firms were penalized for breaching this policy by the withholding of work, while others were not.

Sometimes the argument put forward for this move away from the traditional even-handedness is that it is intended to improve industrial efficiency; but far more often in practice it has been motivated by the social justice of preserving jobs.

It would be foolish (as well as vain) to condemn all these manifestations of collective or social justice. Town and country planning legislation certainly does not extinguish all individual rights. Similarly, few would want to revert to the Combination Acts and prevent any possibility of collection action by the unions. Over the years unions have enhanced the legitimate freedoms of their members, and indeed of other workers, by changing their status from something not altogether unlike that of chattels to that of free men. This has been achieved both through legislation and through collective industrial action, securing on the one hand the rights of consultation, of peaceful picketing, of health and safety at work, of pensions, and on the other hand gaining better pay and conditions generally. This process has, however, reached a stage at which the unions seem in some respects to have moved on from securing their own members' freedom to hindering the freedom of others. I come in a later chapter to the broad question of the political power of the unions; here it is enough to point to the problems of the closed shop, to aggressive picketing, and to the unions' claim that they alone have the right to represent employees. It is here that collective action begins to infringe the deeper rights of the individual.

What about anti-discrimination legislation and positive discrimination? Again it seems reasonable to ensure legally the rights of women and coloured people to be considered equally for jobs and to receive equal pay. I certainly think it right in principle that areas with special need should receive special resources. But when it comes to 'affirmative action' in the shape of selecting for college places applicants from particular ethnic groups who have done less well than other applicants, as in the Bakke case in America, justice is not being served. As in the bussing cases, resentments are easily aroused which can only harm race relations. And even with positive discrimination in favour of inner cities or other deprived areas, one cannot meet all the needs of everywhere; a policy of putting up the rates in the counties in order to help the cities creates as well as alleviates hardship.

Collective and social justices can therefore mean individual injustice. But what about the role of the state, which so often serves as the agent of collective and social justice? In an article in *New Society* ('The future of the state: why it will grow', 2 October 1975) Robert Skidelsky wrote:

> Before we can answer the question: what role will the state have in the future? we must try to work out an answer to another one: will the things people most want require more or less state intervention to secure?

He continued,

> What are these things? People require protection for their lives and property. They require the opportunity to earn a living, and a certain security of employment. They expect their living standards to go up, and life to become more just. . . .

Then he concludes that the increasing role of the state has not been the result of volition or conspiracy. It has come about largely because the things people have most wanted have all required much greater public intervention than was the case in the nineteenth century: 'What does seem to me certain is that collective efforts to secure social goals will increasingly replace individual ones'.

No one will deny that there is increasing public intervention in almost every field. But is it really true that the state has proved successful in meeting the goals that Skidelsky sets out? There are increasing reasons to doubt this. Even in the realms of protection—one would have thought the longest-standing and most fundamental area of state activity (indeed near-monopoly) —the effectiveness of the state has become more and more dubious, as crime and violence mount; and more and more people have turned to private security measures and agencies to protect themselves and their property; and those who have done so have included public bodies, like airports and art galleries, as well as private citizens.

But what about the opportunity to earn a living and security of employment? Obviously Keynesianism and the full employment policy have played a large part here, as indeed have various forms of employment protection legislation and ever increasing state job subsidies. More and more it may be argued that these policies have led to inefficient and uncompetitive industry, and that while jobs may be saved by subsidies or reflation, jobs will also be lost by the consequent poor productivity and inflation. And nowhere have productivity problems been more severe than in those industries controlled by the state—steel, Leyland Motors, the railways and so on. Certainly jobs are provided, but at what price in terms of poor economic performance and lack of resources to invest more constructively, whether in industry or the social services?

Above all it is doubtful whether state intervention is effective in improving living standards justice. It is not only that employment (and tax) policies tend to produce a poorer overall economy, so that there is less to distribute. It seems almost inevitable that the massive scale of state enterprise produces bureaucracy, poor human relations and all sorts of incompetence, particularly when there is no effective profit motive to provide a spur to efficiency. Socialists themselves are worried by this problem, but except for a few rather desultory ideas about

workers' cooperatives and factory autonomy they have no
answer to it.

Skidelsky's view is that our problems will inevitably lead to
still more state intervention. Indicative planning is failing, so we
will have to go on to full-scale planning. Full employment inevitably leads to inflation; therefore the permanent control of
wages and prices is inescapable. Already the Keynesian state is
being replaced by the corporate state (which I shall discuss in
the next chapter), with collective decision-making in the economic field shared between government and the major producers.

Yet it is evident that the bulk of the working population are
angry at the fall in living standards, particularly if they have
children. There are important external reasons for this—the rise
in energy prices and the state of the world economy; but internal
factors loom large as well. After all Germany is also subject to
world trends, and does not even have her own oil; yet her
economy has performed vastly better. But it is not just that there
is great dissatisfaction: there is also, contrary to what Skidelsky
argued in 1975, a growing belief—even to some extent among
Labour ministers—that it is not more public ownership that we
need, but tax cuts, incentives and stimulus to small businesses in
particular. All but the staunchest socialists must have doubts
about creating more British Steels or Leylands. A dose of increased economic freedom, in the market sense, looks more and
more likely to provide that greater economic freedom that comes
comes with more spending power.

There is also disillusionment with the ability of the unions to
secure higher living standards for their members. Union participation in government incomes policies and lower real earnings
are two reasons. The failure of some much publicized industrial
action to secure its objectives is another. At the same time those
firms that do not get caught up in the public ritual of aggressive
unionism and industrial action are often those where pay settle-
ments tend to be the best. This is a complicated matter, which
has much to do with the underlying viability of different industries; nevertheless, I suspect that disenchantment is growing.

Some believe that state and collective action are likely to be
instrumental in securing equality in the creation and sharing of
wealth. I will say only that a more equal sharing of wealth has

only limited attraction if the system produces less wealth overall than would otherwise be the case. Only among the stauncher socialists of the Titmuss school does it seem better for all to be poorer but more equal rather than richer but less equal.

But justice is not solely a matter of economics. One cannot improve on Paul Johnson's deservedly famous essay (*New Statesman*, 9 September 1977), 'Farewell to the Labour Party', with its attack on the way in which individualism has been subordinated to collectivism, the closed shop been allowed to become a tyranny, compromise permitted with union violence and law-breaking and corporatism allowed to spread. As he puts it, 'in a system of belief where conscience has been collectivized, there is no dependable barrier along the highway which may ultimately lead to Auschwitz and Gulag'.

But another, less dramatic article from someone who is still at the time of writing a Labour MP is also very much to the point. In 'Time for Labour to forget some of its past' (*The Times*, 9 February 1976) Bryan Magee pointed out that in the past

> as individuals the majority were powerless. Their only hope of widespread improvement lay with collective action and organised social provision. So the working class organisations that grew up in these circumstances—most important of all the trade unions—developed collectivist notions of democracy almost as a matter of course.

He continued,

> This conception of democracy lives on in the trade union movement though not in isolation. Both its cause and justification— the powerlessness, poverty and ignorance of the individual working man—are fast disappearing. As a result, this approach which in the past was benign and made constructive achievements possible, is decreasingly applicable and is fast becoming a threat to human rights.

As Magee points out,

> the Anglo-Saxon notion of democracy, deriving chiefly from Locke, has always been centrally concerned with the individual

—with protecting his life, his liberty, his pursuit of happiness, *against* the majority, or the government, or any other group more powerful than he is.

These two conceptions of democracy co-exist within the Labour movement; but, says Magee, 'Conditions now demand that the Anglo-Saxon tradition take full possession of the field.' In effect he joins Paul Johnson in refuting Hugh Scanlon's comment that 'Liberty, in my view, is conforming to majority opinion'.

Johnson and Magee are right. A blatant illustration of their point was British Rail's dismissal without compensation of men who had served in some cases for decades because they refused to join a union after a closed shop was brought in. Skidelsky himself commented at the end of the article I have quoted that 'we may easily end up with the worst possible state—one that combines maximum repression with maximum inefficiency'; and argued that 'History has set political theory a new challenge'. I do not claim that this book provides a grand new political theory. It is more concerned with reassessing the relevance of old truths to the modern context. The underlying assumption is that both personal and economic freedom need to be enhanced, and that collective freedom or overriding emphasis on social justice may stand in their way. My stress is on the special role of Parliament in safeguarding individual freedom.

3

Corporatism and the Unions

To some Conservatives, the great problem with power in Britain today is an overmighty Commons—Lord Hailsham's 'elective dictatorship'. The power of the Commons raises important issues, to which I shall turn in the next chapter. But most Conservatives, and most apolitical citizens, have, I suspect, a greater concern: not that Parliament is too powerful, but that it is not powerful enough, at least when challenged by the forces of organized labour. The trauma of February 1974 went deep, and every Conservative MP knows that the most searching political question of the years that followed was 'how would *you* cope with the unions?'

It will be argued that the unions do not represent the only significant economic or industrial force; and of course this is true. Capitalism is not dead, nor wholly manipulated by the state. Multinational companies make decisions that can influence the prosperity of one region or even country against another. Boards of directors can create or terminate jobs, they can invest or not invest. They can also disregard so-called voluntary incomes policies, and other national norms or economic policies.

There are also increasing signs of the growth of an 'unofficial economy', whose operations are designed to evade the hand of government. Transactions are made in cash, so that the taxman does not know what is happening; and very often the work is 'moonlighting'—either a second job or a first job for people drawing unemployment benefits. No one can say how large an element in our society this is; but clearly the existence of these and other forms of tax evasion at all levels of society represent a

19

significant diminution of the state's economic power, as well as a considerable moral problem.

Nevertheless, neither boardrooms nor freebooters represent so formidable a challenge to the parliamentary system as do the unions. It may be that managements have, by not investing more, sometimes failed to respond to government pleas for more investment; but that, so long as we have any semblance of a free economy, hardly rates as defiance, let alone law breaking. Multinationals are normally particularly careful to go along with government, conscious of their own exposed position. And the freebooters, significant though they are, are probably too fragmented to constitute a true power or force in society. Most of us know that the unions represent far the strongest alternative source of power to that which is supposed to lie at Westminster and Whitehall. Certainly the Confederation of British Industry has never seemed to have the muscle of its union counterparts.

Moreover, in Westminster the unions have a direct political impact which no other group can match. They are partners with the Parliamentary Labour Party in the Labour movement as a whole. They have a vital role as paymasters to the movement; they wield massive voting power; they occupy seats on the National Executive of the Labour Party. And, as I have argued already, they are part of a party which does not see democracy simply in parliamentary terms. Whatever the exact relationship between Labour ministers and the Labour conference may be— and so far Prime Ministers have generally followed Attlee in preserving their primary obligation to Parliament and thus the people as a whole—the party outside Parliament is an important power element in the Labour movement, and the unions in turn are an important, indeed crucial, element in that. As the history of Sir Harold Wilson's 1966–70 government showed, the unions were able effectively to veto the proposals for reform of industrial relations that government attempted to launch. Significantly, a number of present generation union leaders make no bones about the fact that they hold more power where they are than if they were in Parliament.

For the unions, power therefore lies quite legitimately not only in the parliamentary ballot box, but also in the union ballot box and the party conference vote. And behind this is an ethos—which is expressed from time to time—which holds that the history of the union movement has proved that the unions cannot always wait for Parliament to legislate, and that unions have rights which may justify them in defying the law of the land. The affair of the five dockers and the 'Shrewsbury Two' were instances of this. In the first case, it was argued among other things that unionists should simply not be imprisoned; in the other, that the law of conspiracy was bad law, and should not be observed—an argument which was also applied to the 1971 Industrial Relations Act and to the court which it set up.

It is important to be fair here. In spite of what I have just said, there is in the union movement a considerable commitment to parliamentary democracy. After all, the union movement in earlier days chose to work through Parliament and its own party in Parliament. It has also a respect for decisions made by majority vote. It would be quite wrong to suggest that the unions as a whole are engaged in a campaign to destroy Parliament. Nor have the unions normally failed to cooperate with Conservative governments. Moreover, the unions generally have a respect for the law, and most unionists do not want to break it. Indeed looking back on the troubled years between 1970 and 1974 it may even be debated as to how often in fact the law was actually broken by unions in the *causes célèbres* of those times, and also whether there was not some failure on the part of government or the law enforcement agencies to uphold the law (which may be an encouragement to breaking it). The mass picketing at Saltley certainly appears illegal, but the police gave way. The affair of the five imprisoned dockers still needs some unravelling. It is not proven that the miners' strike of 1973–74 actually broke the law, for the question did not reach the courts—though clearly the claim broke the legally enforceable pay code.

If it is true, however, that the bulk of the trade union movement is normally committed to parliamentary government and the rule of law as we have known them, the fact remains that the unions have acquired an overall power that seems disproportionate for one, albeit important, sector of the community. For the most part, this power rests on the perfectly legal and proper right to withold one's labour. However, that right is sometimes complicated by the existence of incomes policies which do not

deny the right to strike but make the *object* of strike action
(normally more pay) either illegal—when there is a statutory
control—or at least contrary to government policy, when there
is a voluntary policy. In addition, the right to withold one's
labour is buttressed by various factors, including financial support for strikers or their families through supplementary benefits
and tax rebates, a reluctance by the authorities to use alternative methods of keeping essential services going, and—as I have
indicated already—picketing that sometimes goes beyond the
basic role of persuasion towards blockade and intimidation.
Moreover, the belief that public services will always be bailed
out by the government has allowed their employees to operate
without any very strong fear that if they press industrial action
too far their jobs may disappear. All in all, the balance in free
collective bargaining has tipped in recent years towards the
union.

But the problem is not just one of strikes, or even of the
arguably more serious way in which unions have often acted to
allow their members to work less hard and less productively
when they are at work. The unions have moved from an essentially defensive role concerned with protecting and enhancing
the direct interests of their members to being a power in the
political field, and even a quasi-constitutional body. (Some
would say that in moving into the political arena union leaders
have simultaneously lost touch with their members, leaving a
vacuum often filled by the shop stewards.) Even though the
Bullock version of 'industrial democracy' may be blocked for
the time being, act after act now gives unions powers. More
important, incomes policies in particular have converted the
unions into an Estate of the Realm in a way which would have
surprised earlier union leaders, and, incidentally, would have
appalled a parliamentarian like Aneurin Bevan, who said in the
Commons on 28 April 1944 (Col 1061) speaking specifically of a
deal between Ernest Bevin and the TUC: 'I have protested, on
more than one occasion, about the Government going behind
the back of Parliament, and reaching understandings with outside bodies, and then presenting Parliament with a *fait accom-
pli*'. What would he have made of the Social Contract?

It is doubtful if the public or most of the press ever fully
realized the constitutional development which resulted from the

Social Contract. On more than one occasion Parliament has had to accept without possibility of amendment statements issued by the TUC which were incorporated into white papers in turn given statutory force. Indeed, incomes policy between 1975 and 1977 rested on this procedure, which went far beyond the so-called 'tripartism' of Mr Heath's government. Apart from anything else, the Social Contract was essentially a bipartite deal which left the CBI more or less out in the cold, whistling to keep its spirits up. Worse still, in 1976, 1977, and 1978 the Government did not even put the specific terms of its incomes policies to the House of Commons for a vote.

The fraught question of prices and incomes policy—the problem of inflation, unemployment, and poor productivity—has in fact become embedded in the crucial constitutional question of our time: is it inevitable that power has moved, and will move, into arenas other than the House of Commons?

The question has a long history. It has recently had a very interesting airing in Sir Ian Gilmour's important *Inside Right* (Hutchinson, 1977), as well as in the burst of interest in arguments as to whether we are moving towards a form of corporate state or corporatism, triggered off especially by a series of articles by R. E. Pahl and J. T. Winkler.

Gilmour and Pahl and Winkler present rather different views of what corporatism means, but both views are in a sense versions of how our system of government has responded (and, in Gilmour's case, should respond) to the fact of extra-Parliamentary power and the need either to control it or to work out a modus vivendi with it. The Social Contract was, in its way, another version of this response.

Gilmour's view is that corporatism (which is not, be it said, necessarily the same thing as the corporate state) has a long tradition in England, and is not opposed to either Conservatism or reasonable freedom. Indeed, he argues that those who oppose corporatism have been the totalitarians, to whom 'interest groups are anathema' (p. 244). He goes on: 'Conservatives are on the other side. They are aware of the corporatist tradition in England. "The representatives who appeared in Parliament", wrote Maitland, "were not representative of inorganic collections of individuals, they represented shires and boroughs" '. Gilmour, if I understand him correctly, sees corporations as elements in a pluralist society, where power is diffused and the problems of the overload on government are thereby diminished. We have 'to recognize the power of the trade unions and other producer groups and to try to work with them through consultative procedures, called in Germany and France "concerted action", as suggested in the Conservative Party document *The Right Approach*.' He goes on to argue the case—to which I come back later—for a public industrial forum, based on the NEDC, where incomes policy and so on could be thrashed out.

Gilmour also suggests (p. 245) that

> The degree of corporatism in a country is determined not by the presence or absence of corporate institutions but by the nature and extent of corporate power. An ill man does not become healthy by refusing to recognise his illness, nor does he become more ill if his illness is diagnosed and treated. He may even be cured. Despite the great strength of producer groups in Britain, especially the trade unions, Britain is less well endowed with organisations of cooperation than other countries and with the traditions of communication needs to make them work. Moreover the British party system and the centralisation of the country have placed the making of nearly all political decisions in Whitehall. The deference the executive used to pay to parliament has disappeared in the last few years. Parliament can still not be separated from the executive; nevertheless any sharing of power—indeed even of thought—with producer groups would, if anything, be even more a loss of power by Whitehall than by Westminster. In reality, of course, it would not be a loss of power by either. It would merely be the recognition of loss of power—a very different thing.

In arriving at this view, Gilmour seems to have had in mind an article by Mr James Douglas, 'The Overloaded Crown' (*British Journal of Political Science* 6, 483–505), which in turn was influenced by Professor Ghita Ionescu's *Centripetal Politics* (Hart-Davis, MacGibbon, 1975). Douglas talks of the central theme of the book; 'the division of power in modern societies leads to the neutralization of power by power which is tantamount to powerlessness' (p. 120). But, says Douglas, Ionescu is conscious that it is not strictly the *division* of power that is harmful—it may indeed by useful that the centurion and the priest each has his own defined field of authority—but the *conflict* of power. This leads him to find the solution in a concept that is almost totally absent in our system (and in our language), that of the 'concertation' of power extensively used in France and in the European Community, as in the expression *l'economie concertée*.

Douglas goes on to point out that a number of thinkers, including Ionescu, have come to the view that too great a range of decision-making powers is focused on a single agency, the Crown-in-Parliament, which seems to be inadequate for the task. The burden must be spread.

Ionescu himself sums up his view in the introductory chapter to *Centripetal Politics* (p. 11):

British representative government, while continuing to function regularly, nevertheless would accept the double *partnership* which the social, political and economic processes of the industrial-technological societies by now so very clearly require. One potential and necessary partnership is with the corporate forces of society—social contracts with the trade unions, economic contracts with the enterprises, national contracts with the regions—thus creating a mixed representative-corporate kind of government. The other is with the European Community, creating a mixed national-supranational government. British representative government would therefore continue to be at the centre of British decision-making, but it would work with other centres from which decisions concerning Britain would (indeed actually now do) originate.

This puts in a nutshell Professor Ionescu's belief that we need a dynamic centripetalism to counter the risk that society is falling apart owing to lack of consensus and the strength of centrifugal forces, whether industrial, regional, or (presumably) ethnic or cultural.

Pahl and Winkler take a rather different view of what is happening. In their *Times* article of 26 March 1976 ('Corporatism in Britain') they wrote: 'We see corporatism as a comprehensive economic system in which the state directs and controls predominantly privately-owned business according to four principles: unity, order, nationalism, and success'. But that needs to be supplemented (as I think Pahl and Winkler agree) by something implying the binding in of corporations or bodies representing particular agglomerations of power or interest into the state machine—though often, ostensibly at least, only at arm's length. These corporations would be given the task of regulating their own members and so long as they deliver the goods they will be allowed a good deal of freedom in their own affairs; but basically they would have to work in the direction laid down by the state. Essentially their functions are delegated to them; they are not primarily conflicting elements within a plural society. In other words, the nation state has overriding power; the corporations have delegated power; the individual is left out in the cold.

One other point of definition seems to me to be helpful. For this I draw on an article by Philippe C. Schmitter, 'Still the Century of Corporatism?' (*Review of Politics*, 1974, Vol. 36, pp. 85–131). He writes,

That most original and stimulating of corporate theorists, Mihail Manoilesco, provided the key distinction between two different subtypes. The one he called *corporatisme pur*, in which the legitimacy and functioning of the state were primarily or exclusively dependent on the activity of singular, noncompetitive, hierarchically ordered representative 'corporations'. The second in contrast he called *corporatism subordonné*, in which similarly structured 'corporations' were created by and kept as auxiliary and dependent organs of the state which founded its legitimacy and effective functioning on other bases.

Corporatism subordonné was the pattern of Fascism (in theory if not in practice) and was implicit, for example, in the Italian Charter of Labour of 1927. This charter (which I take from *The Social and Political Doctrines of Contemporary Europe*, Michael Oakeshott, Cambridge 1939) stresses that the nation is

an organic whole having life, purposes and means of action superior in power and duration to those of the individuals, single or associated, of which it is composed. It is a moral, political and economic unity. . . . (Article I).

Article III says that

> Occupational or syndical organisation is free; but only the
> juridically recognised syndicate which submits to the control of
> State has the right to represent legally the entire category of
> employers or workers for which it is constituted, in safeguarding
> its interests *vis-à-vis* the State and other occupational associa-
> tions, in making collective contracts of work binding on all the
> members of the category, in levying contributions and exercis-
> ing over its members functions delegated to it in the national
> interest.

Private enterprise is favoured as the method of production, but,

> being an activity of national interest, the entrepreneur is res-
> ponsible to the State for his organisation. (Article VII.)

The exclusive role that this charter gives to the unions is
echoed in recent Labour employment legislation, while Labour
governments have shown a strong preference for working
through employers' bodies and other corporate associations.
There are also elements of this approach in the views of what
might be termed One Nation Conservatives (far removed from
Fascism) like the pre-war Harold Macmillan, Edward Heath
and Peter Walker—politicians who distrust traditional capitalist
or market economics and stress the need to avoid conflict in
society. These Conservatives seem to share the view that classi-
cal, liberal individualism is incompatible with the effective
ordering of a complicated society in a complicated world: the
state must take the lead in promoting harmony, not simply hold
the ring. And of course this attitude is very far from being exclusively Conservative: there are plenty of Liberals and social
democrats who take the same kind of approach. (I will leave
on one side the similarities between Fascism and the more
totalitarian left-wing creeds). The Italian Charter of Labour
goes much further in imposing state regulation than would
recent moderate British politicians; but as Winkler puts it in his
paper in the *British Journal of Law and Society* (Vol. 2, No 2),

> by the closing stages of the Conservative government, the then
> Secretary of State for Trade and Industry, Peter Walker, was

explicating what amounted to a tentative theory of corporatism.
The government was developing 'a new form of interventionism'.
in which the role of the State was to harness capitalism to the interest
of all and the role of business was to 'make a profit for Britain'.

Perhaps I should point out that in an article in *The Daily
Telegraph* (16 August 1976) Mr Walker rejected a perpetual
incomes policy on the grounds that 'It would do much to create
the Corporate State; even so, I would argue that one of his preferr-
ed measures—a *statutory* requirement for postal ballots or secret
ballots for union elections—smacks of corporatism.

Indeed, it raises one of the key questions which we must face:
how far should the state go in regulating the internal conduct of
trade unions, and for that matter, of business? No one could say
that the 1971 Industrial Relations Act was an attempt to destroy
the trade union movement: it was much more an attempt to
define and regulate the role of the unions in society. The act
could, however, be said to have diverged from the classic free
market or pluralist view of society, which implies that the state
has a duty to regulate what might be called the external behaviour of trade unions, employers' associations and so on, but not
the way in which they actually run themselves. Intervention in
their internal running is in a sense an acknowledgement that
unions and employers' associations are a part of the government of the country, or an estate of the realm.

Is the whole apparatus of recent interventionism—the two
Industry Acts, Government-CBI-TUC tripartitism, the selective distribution of favours to failing companies, the various
forms of incomes policy, and so on—correctly seen as part of a
corporatist tendency? This is a hugely complicated question, but
I must say that it seems to me that this apparatus may not be
corporatist *tout court*, but that it lends itself to corporatism in
the second of the two patterns defined by Manoilesco, *corporatisme subordonné*. Planning agreements, for example, could
well have followed from the Charter of Labour if the Italian
fascist government had felt that private industry was not quite
doing its bit. More significantly, perhaps, the tripartite talks between government, unions and management of recent years (sometimes but not always conducted within the framework of NEDC)
have at times represented a step in the corporatist direction.

Let me emphasize the word *step*. What happened under Mr
Heath in 1972–3 was certainly not fully fledged corporatism of
either pattern. Nevertheless, Heath was interested in a somewhat changed pattern of parliamentary government. On these
changes I would like to quote at some length from an article by
Mr David Wood in *The Times* of 7 October 1974, three days
before the general election.

> Mr Heath would create out of the NEDC a national form which,
> under the unblinking eye of the television cameras, would pro-
> vide the exchange and mart for popular political education that
> is, among other things, Parliament's role.
>
> Take Mr Heath's proposal. Consider its provenance and its
> rationale. The idea springs from Mr Heath's deep conviction
> that the 21 months he spent as Prime Minister in talks with the
> CBI and TUC at 10 Downing Street and Chequers came nearer
> than is popularly understood to establishing a common purpose
> between government, industry and the unions. He saw it, and
> still sees it, as a sustained seminar in which all three parties
> dicovered the minimum terms for cooperations and partnership.
>
> Yet Mr Heath and his economic Ministers knew the educative
> function of the talks was too circumscribed. The small group
> directly involved might see the problem with a fresh eye and
> might even agree on some of the practicable solutions (preferen-
> tial treatment of pensions and the low-paid workers, for
> example), but neither ministers nor trade union leaders could
> march too far ahead of their rank and file, in Parliament or on
> the shop floor. . . .
>
> Then on his recent visit to Washington, Mr Heath heard from
> President Ford how, on the initiative of Democrat leaders, the
> two sides of American industry, leading economists, and sub-
> stantial politicians were to join in televised discussions to find
> agreement on what was best for the national interest.
>
> Here was Mr Heath's agency for popular education. He saw
> the NEDC as the cadre of a national forum and television, when
> appropriate, as Everyman's night school. Here lay a path of
> escape from the sterile partisan dog-fight and the chopping and
> changing of policies that is Parliament; here the representatives
> of the real interests within the nation could be seen and heard
> speaking for themselves in a practical, civilised, and rational
> way. . . .
>
> What does he prescribe as the role for his national forum? As
> a first task, he says it would have presented to it a thorough and

detailed analysis of the national accounts. Agreement would be sought on Britain's need to meet the crisis, and that would lead, he suggests, to a consensus 'on the aggregate totals anticipated to be right for the economy, for personal incomes, profits, investment, and public spending'. It is government with politics taken out.

Here is a plain substitution of the national forum for what is theoretically one of the principle functions of the Executive in Parliament. And what virtue did Mr Heath claim for his national forum over Parliament? When a rather troubled journalist, a former right-wing Conservative candidate, asked where Parliament stood in the scheme of things, Mr Heath answered that Parliament was not televised; and in saying that his implication was unmistakable—that he now thinks that Parliament, cut off from the people and living perhaps in a spurious world of its own, cannot perform its popular educative function any more than it can now bring into rational discussion the Estates of the Realm. . . .

Mr Heath seemed to have in mind something between the educative and the decision-taking roles of Parliament, though perhaps the essence of the tripartite approach was the creation of a *negotiating* body. Sir Ian Gilmour seems to take the same sort of view. However one defines it, it is a very different style to that of traditional parliamentary democracy.

Whatever exactly Mr Heath may have had in mind, it is unlikely that he would have gone very far in the direction of the cooperative corporatism of Manoilesco's first type. I think he would have envisaged this new form ultimately as a machine to be used by the government, as a way of binding the other parties into a government-led search for an agreed approach to the nation's problems. In a sense he was trying to turn the familiar Disraeli-esque Tory slogan of One Nation into an institutional reality. In doing so, he was of course combining a very generalized principle with some hard-boiled pragmatism: he would not have been concerned with the kind of theorizing that marked the Fascists.

There are other moderate politicians, however, who have gone farther than Mr Heath towards a form of corporatism. The late John Mackintosh MP in a PEP Broadsheet (*Reshaping Britain*, No 548) discussed tripartism and the NEDC and then went on to argue that one reason why Parliament has lost power is because its members are party nominees rather than the actual representatives of an area or group. Few now think that the votes of MPs indicate the positive assent of those they are held to represent, which is why the acceptance of a law by the House of Commons is not now regarded as conveying sufficient legitimacy by itself. But it is of considerable help to the government if the contemporary equivalent of the barons give their assent—if the CBI, the unions or the porfessional associations give their agreement —since they can be held to account and can be expected to secure the cooperation of their members. And if, in the process of consultation, some of the power blocs agree but others do not, then the minority is struggling not merely with the government but with the rest of its peers who are prepared to agree.

He argues that mediaeval parliaments were based on the assumption that there were powerful elements in the country whose understanding and agreement had to be obtained for any common policy to be enforced. He goes on to state the case for a new Upper House of, say, two hundred members. Industry and the unions might nominate forty each; there would be twenty ministers and officials, and the rest would come from recognized pressure groups. Its powers would be very much akin to those of the present House of Lord.

This certainly has a somewhat corporatist look about it; but what about the policies pursued by the Wilson and Callaghan Labour governments, in particular through the various marks of the Social Contract? Here we are coming closer to Manoilesco's *corporatisme pur*.

The Labour government continued to use NEDC—perhaps increasingly; and it continued to consult with the CBI; but the contract between the government/parliamentary arm of the Labour movement and the TUC was the special feature of the post-1974 period. For one thing, it covered much more than economic and industrial matters: social policy was very much a part of it. For another, as I have already indicated, it has left its mark on the statute book.

But the really interesting question about the Social Contract is a kind of 'who, whom?' question. Has it ultimately meant that the unions have become equal partners of the government (a variant of co-operative corporatism); or has it meant that they have ultimately found themselves turned into instruments of government, perhaps in the kind of way indicated in the PEP chapter I have just quoted? Or does the truth lie somewhere between the two?

It is too early to give an answer; but at times it has looked as though the 'sell-out' to the unions might prove to be something rather different; and that pressure might grow in the unions for a reversion to their traditional arm's length bargaining status.

What are we to conclude from this brief sketch of what is, or may have been, happening? Is freedom at risk—and if so, does it matter?

I certainly do not believe that corporatism should be confused with straightforward socialism. Nationalization is not corporatism; though nationalization of the banks or insurance companies would in my view by thoroughly odious, it would not be corporatist. But an increasing tendency to use banks, insurance companies, building societies, other businesses or trade unions as instruments of the state is another matter. It may not represent formal corporatism, or be codified in the way that the Italian Charter of Labour was; but the stronger forms of tripartitism, planning agreements, detailed internal regulation of unions, and so on all seem to me corporatist in tendency. That still leaves us with the question of whether this tendency is wrong: given that people as far from Fascist as Harold Macmillan and John Mackintosh (to name but two) have at times favoured measures which seem to have a corporatist flavour, it is clearly not enough to treat the word 'corporatist' as a word of abuse and leave it at that.

Indeed the Mackintosh/PEP chapter raises one essential question:

some may look back to theories of the corporate state current in the 1930s and ask how far recognition of the power of such groups is a denial of democracy. Clearly, in the sense that these groups recognise that legislative chambers based on 'one person, one vote' are not enough in themselves either to contain all the necessary parties to negotiations or to legitimise all laws, this is true. But if the power in a society is 'lump', then the lumps will remain and the only question is whether their position is to be regularised and institutionalised or left on an informal basis. ... It is better to recognise that the upper house would be a

rough and ready way of collecting the voices of the powerful
... while the Commons remained the true voice of the people,
the consumers and the taxpayers.

The PEP pamphlet's scheme allowed for sovereignty to
remain ultimately with the Commons. But would it? Would the
upper house—conscious of the power it represented and more
self-confident than the present unrepresentative House of Lords
—accept the will of the Commons in the way that the peers do
today, or even in the way a popularly elected Second Chamber,
operating under clearly defined limits, would accept it? And
what about the alternative of tripartite bargaining about a
'national dividend', whether or not conducted in front of the
television cameras? Even if the result had to be ratified by
Parliament, would Parliament find it easy to stand out against
the tripartite deal?

Be realistic, we are told: recognize where power lies, and then
try to contain it where necessary. But 'containment' implies not
only formal recognition but the granting of additional power to
already powerful bodies. Blocs of power will inevitably exist in
society, but the great need is for an all-powerful Parliament to
represent the totality of individuals and see that the over-
mighty are kept in check. Any upper house based on interest
and pressure groups would be arbitrary in its composition;
hosts of people would be unrepresented as under tripartitism,
and how much legitimacy we should give the self-appointed
pressure groups is debatable. (In some respect we have gone too
far already.) Of course, pressures and interests are represented
in Parliament—but that is the result of a choice to which every
elector can contribute. Respect for Parliament may be low, but I
doubt if respect for a system more openly based on the broker-
age of power groups would be higher. Meanwhile any 'reform'
—be it an Industrial Parliament, a super-Neddy, or referenda—
which confirms the drift of power from Parliament to industrial interests will serve only to weaken the authority of Parliament in general. As Parliament weakens, so the strength and
legitimacy of bodies like the unions will grow. And who can
say that giving the producer interests greater power will make
our industry more efficient and more competitive—which
remains Britain's greatest need?

The *trahison des clercs* today is fatalism: political science and sociology are great breeders of predestination. The rights and opportunities of the individual are diminishing in the process. This is the inevitable tendency of corporatism in the Pahl–Winkler, or *corporatisme subordonné*, sense; and one may glimpse it spreading into Parliament itself, with the idea that the state should become the paymaster of the political parties.

But it is not only the state's use the corporations as its agents that we should reject: Ionescu's concept of centripetalism and concertation is also potentially damaging. His notion of partnership with the corporate forces of society—'social contracts with the unions, economic contracts with the enterprises, national contracts with the regions'—may seem a realistic way of trying to hold society together, but it is very hard to get the balance of the partnership right. The social contract may at one moment entail the unions dictating to the government; at the next they may be trapped by the government. Economic contracts with the enterprises look equally questionable, and calculated to worsen the red tape, inflexibility and over-manning that are the all too frequent products of interventionism. National contracts with the regions also have dangers which I shall discuss: regional governments, at whatever level, may simply end up as agents of the state.

It is far better that government have clearcut and strong powers over a clearly defined but limited field. The same should apply to local government over a lesser field. Beyond that we should see the corporations as acceptable members of a plural society, but with the law and the courts and Parliament there to make sure that they do not use their strength oppressively.

How does this apply to the crucial question of prices and incomes? As far as possible they should be left to the market and the bargaining process. But if we must have an imposed incomes policy, that must be decided by Parliament: the government may *consult* in formulating the policy, but the decision must lie with Parliament. for only Parliament will be concerned with the interests of the *whole* community. (The idea that a nominated National Consumer Council can do the job of protecting individuals is far-fetched.) Better, however, not to have an imposed incomes policy at all, because of the distortions, anomalies and disincentives to efficiency which incomes policies bring, and because forcing the government to take sides in industrial disputes gravely strains the system. Unfortunately, nationalization makes the latter inevitable, as the government are bound to be in the position of owners; but even here the government should not be more heavily involved than is necessary.

But if we take that view, then we must be sure not only that the consumer is sufficiently protected through monopolies legislation and true competition, but that the collective bargaining system actually works fairly.

As I have said already, it seems doubtful whether it does: the scales have been tipped too far in favour of the unions, by a combination of factors which include supplementary benefits, tax rebates, the greater inter-dependence of essential services, more aggressive picketing and sympathetic action, reluctance to take firm steps to keep vital services going, and possibly reduced fear of unemployment.

Are we prepared to tackle these issues, and if so how? I certainly do not wish to see massive confrontation over these matters; nor is there any point in, for instance, changing the law affecting supplementary benefits or the system of paying tax rebates unless the result is actually likely to reduce strikes. (There may be other ways in which the financial disadvantages of being on strike might increase.) Nevertheless, any society must protect itself, and *if* it is clear that the balance of collective bargaining is distorted by public policies which make it possible to prolong strikes excessively, then those policies will have to be changed.

As for controlling picketing, the existing law would, I believe, be adequate if it were properly enforced: aggressive picketing, mass picketing and blockading seem clearly illegal. I doubt whether a new law trading, for example, a limitation on numbers of demonstrators for a right to stop vehicles would really bring about a more satisfactory state of affairs. It is basically a matter of will.

Most important of all, however, all sides clearly must accept the right and duty of government to keep essential services going. This duty applied during the firemen's strike of 1977, when virtually no one disputed it: but it should be just as true of a power strike, a sewage stike or a hospital strike. One view is that workers in these essential services should be denied the right to strike, as policemen and soldiers are and power workers were, with the quid pro quo of their pay being indexed. That may be difficult to achieve; in which case it becomes the duty of government to be prepared to put in the personnel needed to keep these services going at a tolerable level, and where necessary to keep such trained personnel in readiness. Emergency powers really should make it possible to cope with an emergency; and if effective action is taken without drama, the public will support it.

Here we are talking about a last resort; for the most part, the traditional bargaining system should be capable of dealing with pay determination. Of course, every time the public sector is enlarged the problem becomes more difficult. It must be made clear to the managements of nationalized industries what financial support, if any, they may expect, and then they must be left to negotiate within that framework. The same should apply to local government. With the civil service, the government is bound to be directly involved. It must ultimately be able to take a view as to what it can afford, rather than leaving the whole matter to an independent mechanism.

All this, no doubt, is easier said than done. Nevertheless, there are signs that the unions may be passing the apogee of their power. Not only has public opinion swung more strongly against aggressive union action, but also members of unions (especially in the private sector) may become increasingly sceptical about the value of traditional industrial action and trade union activity as a means of winning more real wealth or a better life. As unions take on board more white collar workers, they may find—as has happened with Clive Jenkins' ASTMS —that their members become less interested in nationalization, and more interested in the restoration of differentials, incentives, and tax reductions. And this is not confined to white collar workers. Thus Frank Chapple of the electrical trades union (EEPTU) was quoted in *The Times* of 10 May 1978, as saying that if the government tried 'to inflict egalitarian policies' on power workers it would face a battle. Who know—unions may even come to see that the only road to real wealth lies through improved productivity? Moreover, the new union members— many of them Tory or Liberal—may not be keen on intensifying the notion that there are two sides of industry (the keystone of much of the Labour government's policies between 1974 and 1976) and lean rather to the belief that in many cases technology and social attitudes are making this view of society obsolescent.

It is not my purpose here to write about economic and industrial policy in any detail: my interest is in who should make what decisions. I do not believe that government should be involved in the business of settling pay at every level: it is an impossible task, in terms of fairness and economic effectiveness and in the strains that it may impose on the body politic. Nor do I believe that the job should be performed by corporatist mechanisms. The two sides of industry should not be given collectively the job of helping to formulate and then police a policy for incomes. Nor should the government bargain as an equal party with the two sides of industry to achieve an agreed settlement, to be imposed by whatever means. I do accept that under certain conditions government through Parliament may have to enact an incomes policy, and of course in achieving that there is no reason why governments should not talk to the CBI, the TUC or anyone else. But the ultimate decision must be that of an unfettered Parliament.

Has Parliament the means of making such decisions effectively? An industrial parliament is unacceptable because it places too much power in the hand of producers (and a limited selection of producers at that); the glorified Neddy suffers from the same defect; and both tend to reinforce the drift to collectivism that is weakening individual freedom. If management or unions feel that there should be more managers or unionists in one or other House, there is no reason why they should not win places there. (I discuss in a later chapter my views on how the second chamber might be reshaped.) The important thing is that in none of its forms does corporatism offer the right answer to the problem of union power; fundamentally corporatism is never concerned with the individual but only with the collectivity, never with the consumer but only the producer. The task must lie with Parliament; but none of us in Parliament can be sure that the way in which we handle these matters is at present as effective as it should be. Parliament must heal itself before it can heal others.

4

Over-mighty Commons?

'Under all the formality, the antiquarianism, the shams of the British constitution, there lies an element of power which has been the true source of its life and growth. This secret source of strength is the absolute omnipotence, the sovereignty, of Parliament'. Dicey's words convey the essence of our constitution as it used to be seen. Today this idea is being challenged by outside forces which claim a strength and legitimacy of their own. Parliament may still be formally sovereign, but it is not omnipotent, especially in the face of industrial power. In some ways Parliament is too weak.

But there is another view that has to be considered—the view that Parliament, or rather the Commons, constitutes what Lord Hailsham calls an 'elective dictatorship' and that the dominance of the majority party (normally backed by only a minority of the electorate) is excessive. Is it right that the Commons should be able to churn out legislation for which there is almost certainly no majority support in the country, that there should be no written constitutional restraints on its actions, that the courts should have no power to declare enacted laws invalid, and that the power of the Lords to act as a brake on the Commons should be so circumscribed? These questions have all taken their places on the agenda of political discussion after a long absence. Lord Hailsham and Lord Scarman in particular have opened up the argument, reinforced by electoral reformers, devolutionists, campaigners for a Bill of Rights, advocates of the referendum, supporters of more participation and power to the grassroots, and, of course, in addition, membership of the EEC has serious implications for the sovereignty of Parliament.

Hailsham's views have been expressed in a series of articles in *The Times* in May 1975, his 1976 Richard Dimbleby Lecture,

of which substantial extracts were published in *The Times* of
15 October 1976, and more recently in his book *The Dilemma
of Democracy* (Collins, 1978). His conclusion is that our constitution is wearing out. Its central defects are gradually coming to
outweigh its merits, and its central defects consist in the absolute
powers we confer on our sovereign body, and the concentration
of those powers in an executive government formed out of one
party which does not always fairly represent the popular will.
In spite of the priceless asset of the constitution's 'immemorial
antiquity, which with its power of continuous growth gives it a
prestige and mystique not shared by any other nation in the
world', we have moved towards 'a totalitarianism which can
only be altered by a systematic and radical overhaul of our
constitution' (Dimbleby Lecture).

The ingredients of the problem include a continuous enlarge-
ment of the scale and range of government; the vast mass of
legislation; the strength of the whips, the party caucus and the
Executive; the weakness of the House of Lords; the passing of
the power of dissolution firmly into the hands of the Prime
Minister; the 'wholly unconstitutional doctrines of the mandate
and manifesto'; and the willingness of governments with only
minority support in the country to impose very controversial
measures. Hailsham argues that 'what is ultimately unfair about
our present constitution is that it gives absolute power when all
reason and experience tend to show that unlimited powers are
intolerable'.

Lord Scarman's critique, expressed in his famous 1974
Hamlyn Lectures (*English Law—the New Dimension*, Stevens,
1974), is perhaps restrained by the fact that he is judge rather
than politician. Nevertheless, it is formidable. His essential
question: 'Is English Law capable of further growth within the
limits of the common law system?' or 'Has the common law
reached the end of the road?' He describes how in effect the
customary common law has more and more been supplemented
by statute law. As Lord Simonds put it, 'if a gap is disclosed, the
remedy lies in an amending Act'. The judges do not make law,
though they lay it down; equally, Parliament legislates in the
context of the 'all-pervading customary law'.

But the system is under challenge—from the international
human rights movement and the Common Market; from the

concept of social justice which holds that a framework of freedom for individuals to work out their own destinies is not
enough, and that the law should be loaded in favour of the
weak; from the challenge of attitudes to the environment which
hold that the traditional concentration on property is not
enough; from the challenge in the field of industrial relations;
and from the challenge of devolution, which calls for some
written constitution and a mechanism for settling disputes
about *vires*.

Underlying all that Scarman says one may perceive his feeling
that the common law is no longer a sufficient defence of our
freedoms. He seems sympathetic to the point that the omnipotence of Parliament has not always been unchallenged. He
quotes Oliver Cromwell's remark that

> In every Government there must be Somewhat Fundamental,
> Somewhat like a Magna Charter, which should be standing, be
> unalterable. . . . That Parliaments should not make themselves
> perpetual is a Fundamental. Of what assurance is a law to pre-
> vent so great an evil if it lie in the same legislature to un-law it
> again?

Scarman concludes that we need a new *written* constitution
settlement together with a supreme court with powers to invalidate unconstitutional legislation; we need to accept entrenched
provisions and a Bill of Rights; we need a survey of the balance
in the legal system between judge-made law and statute, possibly
with a move to codification; we need to consider the problem of
administrative law, and in particular the tendency to administer
social justice or deal with disputes in the social services, industrial relations, and the environment through separate tribunals
which are not part of a unified legal system. There should be a
continuing review of the law through the Law Commissions.
Most controversially,

> the judge, treating statute no longer as the exception but as the
> basis of the law, will have to adopt the interpretative policy for
> which Lord Denning was once rebuked by Lord Simonds—the
> policy of making good the omissions of Parliament consistently
> with the legislative purpose of the enactment. . . . These greater

powers—startling though they may appear in the context of the existing law—will be fully consistent with the new role assigned to judges as guardians of the constitution.

Both Hailsham and Scarman are, then, clearly deeply discontented with our traditional ways. Although their profession is imbued in custom and tradition, they feel the need now for a major break with the past—a substantially new and written constitution. A growing number of others share their view, whether in whole or in part, though motives vary across the political spectrum.

One particularly vigorous attack on the status quo comes from the electoral reformers. The essence of their case lies in equity, but its practical attraction to many of those who support it lies in the claim that it provides the means for checking extremism, particularly of the kind pursued by Labour in the two years after it came to power in 1974, or that could be pursued in the future if the party were returned to power with an overall majority.

The argument for devolution, to which both Hailsham and Scarman seem sympathetic, represents an attempt not so much to diminish the power of Parliament as to disperse it. Hailsham in particular favours the Liberal approach of a federal United Kingdom, with English regions on a par with Scotland, Wales, and Northern Ireland: 'The interests of regions, minorities, and individuals would be safe-guarded by law, by the provision of a proportionately elected second Chamber, and by the separate regional assemblies'.

The Bill of Rights again is common ground between Hailsham and Scarman, and there is now a considerable body of support for the notion, which I will not set out in detail. But there are divergences of views as to what a Bill of Rights should cover. Should it be essentially concerned with civil liberties, of the kind, for example, for which the National Council of Civil Liberties campaigns? Or should it also embrace freedoms which might be held to have a more strongly political flavour—for instance, freedom for private health provision or private education, freedom to pass on one's possessions, and so on?

The two major existing exemplars—the United Nations Universal Declaration of Human Rights and the European

Convention on Human Rights derived from it—are primarily of a 'civil liberties' nature. But there are ingredients of more partisan significance: the right to join a trade union in the European convention (the UN declaration also included the right *not* to); and at least arguably the right to freedom of choice, especially religious choice, in education. The right not to be discriminated against on grounds of race has also been held to invalidate at least some of the immigration control measures taken by British governments.

The Bill of Rights question is, of course, tied up with other possible constitutional changes—for example, a requirement that legislation involving constitutional changes receives a two thirds majority in one or both Houses of Parliament, or alternatively that it be submitted to a referendum.

The referendum, after years of argument earlier in the century, has now become a part of our political scene. Although it was by and large Conservatives who supported it then, as a means of checking an over-radical Commons bent on controversial constitutional change, and although Conservatives like Lord Hailsham still make the same point today, it is Labour that has actually brought it forward over the EEC and the devolution bills. Ostensibly the argument has been that the people should decide on matters of overriding significance: in fact, of course, in both cases the referendum was designed to resolve an internal Labour Party dilemma. This is not to say, however, that the referendum might not become a legitimate means of expression or decision where matters of sovereignty, or something close to sovereignty, are at stake, as was true of the referendum brought in by Mr Heath's government for Northern Ireland.

The referendum is the most clear-cut new approach to seeking the consent of the people, but in its various shapes and forms 'participation' is another way of achieving the same objective. It is a difficult concept to formalize, at least if it is seen as sharing power with those directly affected by a scheme. In fact power sharing is not compatible with our normal ideas of democratic decision-taking and accountability: the right of being consulted the correct approach; but those who are consulted, as at motorway inquiries, sometimes find it hard to accept that the right to be consulted does not imply the right to have one's views accepted. Nevertheless, the democratic process in this sort of planning matter may well be in need of overhaul.

The air then is thick with clamour for constitutional change of one kind or another. How should we respond? And is it possible to do so from a coherent basis, rather than piecemeal?

I do not fully accept Lord Hailsham's view that we suffer from an over-mighty Commons. As I have argued in the last chapter, the greatest threats today are those which come from alternative sources of power. The strongest check on an elective dictatorship comes from the fact that the next Parliament can reverse its predecessor's decisions. It is only if that ceases to be the case, and Parliament loses its freedom of action, that dictatorship may become entrenched. For this reason, it is necessary both to reassert the supremacy of Parliament against other, sometimes corporatist forces, but also to think hard about improving the effectiveness of Parliament.

Underlying this view is the belief that it is not possible to imagine any other body having the legitimacy which Parliament derives both from its ancient history and the fact that every adult citizen has a say in its composition.

By the same token, the legitimacy of Parliament, and especially the Commons, rests on bipartisan or all-party support. Although there are reservations—the Liberals want to change the electoral system and the nationalist parties want to be out—no party rejects Parliament as it is. Major changes could be a very different matter. In particular, it must be doubted whether the Labour Party would accept the package put forward by Lord Hailsham—which is after all designed to hold Labour in check. That is a desirable enough objective, from both his and my point of view, but it is not a good starting point for reform. In his article in *The Times* of 19 May 1975, Lord Hailsham wrote that one of the reasons which has led him to favour a Bill of Rights is that 'the present Labour Government is persistently proposing legislation under the guise of its doctrine of mandate which would almost certainly be caught by any Bill of Rights legislation however formulated. The most obvious example of this is their trade union legislation'. The closed shop and other challenges to the liberty of the individual are matters of great importance, but I doubt whether it would be wise to deal with them through constitutional rather than ordinary legislation.

(The same would apply to checking the extension of public ownership). To attempt to do so would certainly make the achievement of constitutional reform very much more difficult: the best way to bring such reform about is through as much consensus as is feasible.

Perhaps the most difficult question is how much value to attach to *customary* liberties and relationships, as opposed to formally drafted statutes. It seems to me that Scarman's argument is persuasive and that the Common Law has largely been overtaken by statute law. But there is a less easily defined area, which may nevertheless be important. In an essay published in *New Society* ('Reflections on Liberty', 27 May 1977) the French anthropologist Claude Levi-Strauss argued that

> By placing freedom on what is claimed to be a rational basis one is condemning it to forgo this rich content and thus to undermine its own foundations. For the attachment to freedom is all the stronger when the rights it is asked to protect are based in part on the irrational: they consist of those minute privileges, perhaps negligible inequalities, which while they do not interfere with a general equality nevertheless provide the individual with some firm footholds in his immediate surroundings.
>
> True liberty is the liberty of custom, that is—as the history of France since 1789 proves—a form of liberty against which all theoretical ideas usually considered rational are pitched into battle. . . . Liberty is preserved from within; its foundations are being sapped when people think they can build it from outside.

This is of course an anthropologists' view, a reaction against the formal constitutional legalism of his own country. He quotes Maine's remark, 'The philosophers of France, in their eagerness to escape from what they deemed a superstition of the priests, flung themselves headlong into a superstition of the lawyers'; and clearly the English tradition has more appeal for him. But then, interestingly enough, he says, 'Rousseau wanted to abolish all partial associations within the state; on the contrary a degree of revival of such partial associations offers a lasting way of restoring some health and vigour to our ailing liberties'. This is where the echoes of corporatism come in—a notion which has had more to do with Catholic France than Protestant England.

Yet Levi Strauss' corporatism—if corporatism it be—is very
different from the corporatism that surfaced, for example, under
Vichy. For that sort of corporatism was formal: the corporations were assigned a place within the scheme of things, essentially as instruments of the state. Is his view therefore closer to
the 'pure' corporatism which may lead to corporations bargaining as more or less equal parties with government, as in the
Social Contract? I do not think so: he is talking about something essentially informal, almost undefined and private—a
subtle sort of pluralism.

I suppose that the most striking example of the political power
of custom has once again to be derived from the field of industrial relations. Unlike both Mrs Castle and the 1966–70 Labour
government and Mr Heath's Conservative government, the
Donovan report stressed the conventions and customs of
industrial relations and tended to play down legal solutions such
as enforceable contracts. Indeed, the report seemed more like an
anthropologist's than a lawyer's report.

Of course, one man's freedom is another man's loss of freedom; there may come a time when the law *has* to step in to
protect the individual. This may be done through the courts,
continuing the traditional common law concern for the individual (it is this that has led to the charge that the courts are
anti-union); or it may have to take the form of statute. (It is
becoming more and more apparent that if the unions want to
have their rights enshrined in law they may also have to face
up to laws enshrining other people's rights.) Even so, we should
not hurry to switch from custom to statute in these matters
unless we have no option.

Does that mean that after all I accept corporatism? Only in
this sense: while government and Parliament should be supreme,
they should not seek actively to exercise that supremacy in every
sphere of our life, or to stamp out pluralist decision-making.
Right across our society a mass of relationships, activities and
transactions should normally be no concern of either government or law.

There is therefore still an important place for custom, particularly when the custom has deep roots. Change can become a
self-reinforcing habit: one of the best reasons for not drastically
changing the constitution or the powers of Parliament is that

every time we do so we lose a little of their authority. They can only work with public confidence and too much change and argument about change can serve to diminish this confidence. But equally they must work, and that entails some flexibility. (The great argument for the unwritten constitution is its flexibility.)

The other thing that damages government is evidence that those services which it runs itself are run badly—whether they be armed services, social service, or nationalized industries. We may wish for less government, but we make a great mistake if we accept poor services and low standards in the public sector, and Conservatives should be as much concerned with morale in, say, the health service, as they are about morale in the armed forces.

To sum up, then, our approach to constitutional change should be marked where possible by bi-partisanship; by an acceptance that customs still have their place and that government should not seek omnicompetence, even if in the last resort it is omnipotent; by a reluctance to change for change's sake; an important point that I have not so far stressed—and recognition that there are higher freedoms and principles which no constitutional mechanism should overthrow or breach. It is here especially that custom and tradition may be as important as mechanism. Given these principles how should we approach the various proposals for constitutional reform?

Lord Hailsham in his Dimbleby Lecture said: 'I envisage nothing less than a written constitution for the United Kingdom, and by that I mean one that limits the powers of Parliament and provides a means of enforcing these limitations both by political and legal means'. He postulates two Chambers of Parliament, both elected—the Commons as at present, the upper house elected by proportional representation and on a regional basis. Scotland, Northern Ireland, Wales, and the English regions would each have regional assemblies within the framework of a federal constitution. There would be an entrenched Bill of Rights. The respective spheres of influence of Parliament and the assemblies would be defined by law and policed by the ordinary courts. The whole process would be enacted by recommendations from a constitutional convention, followed by a bill and then a referendum, which would confirm the bill and also give separatists a chance to vote to opt out of the United Kingdom.

In some respects I follow Lord Hailsham's proposals; in others I do not. I doubt in particular that we are at the stage to make the leap to a fully-fledged written constitution preceded by a constitutional convention. There is not yet strong enough feeling on all sides in favour of such a development: the Labour Party in particular would be too suspicious of what was intended. Moreover, the situation in Northern Ireland is still too clouded to allow us to commit ourselves to the early restoration of a devolved government as opposed to direct rule; yet a constitutional convention could hardly duck that issue.

Nevertheless, we may be moving almost inexorably in the direction of at least a greater written element in our constitution. We are already parties to the European Convention on Human Rights. We signed it in 1951, and since 1966 have accepted the right of individual petitioning to the European Commission and the compulsory jurisdiction of the European Court. We have not yet, however, incorporated it in our domestic law. For one thing, it is argued that with our tradition no statute is incapable of amendment—yet it is presumably part of the point of the European convention that it should apply to all signatories alike and amendment would defeat this. There is also the difficulty of how to apply the general provisions of a Bill of Rights to the terms of specific statutes existing now or in the future: we are not used to the concept of one Act of Parliament qualifying the provisions of another in this way.

Lord Hailsham would solve this problem by creating a new entrenched written constitution with clear provisions for the circumstances by which its ingredients would be changed. (A two-thirds majority, whether in one or both Houses, and perhaps a referendum, are mechanisms that advocates of a written constitution tend to favour as the requirements for amendment of that constitution.) It may be that we shall have to come to this; but might it not be possible—as the House of Lords Select Committee on a Bill of Rights recommended—simply to enact the European convention as a Bill of Rights in our domestic law and see what happened? This would imply that Parliament would have to restrain itself from making changes to the Bill once it had been passed, and indeed during its passage. As to the

complications that might arise from conflict between the Bill of
Rights and other statutes, it might well be possible to leave
disputes to the courts, with the assumption that they will tend
to be strongly influenced in their judgements by the Bill of
Rights, rather as they have been influenced by the Common
Law.

A Bill of Rights of this kind would be a constitutional inno-
vation (or revival) rather than a part of a written constitution;
that is to say, its force would not be to govern the terms of other
statutes, but rather to try to ensure that the administration conformed to a particular code of conduct in matters affecting the
liberty of the individual. The devolution legislation brings us
more nearly to the reality of a written constitution, in that it
defines certain powers which are to be operated by devolved
governments (even if subject to the ultimate authority of Parliament); and it also calls for the settlement of disputes by the
Judicial Committee of the Privy Council, in effect a constitutional court. There are powerful arguments against the government's devolution scheme—above all, the anomalous position
in which it places Members of Parliament from the different
parts of the UK, with the Scots members able to vote on domestic English, Welsh, and Northern Irish matters, but not on
devolved subjects in their own land. There is indeed a better
approach to the devolution of power from London, which I
shall discuss later. Nevertheless, if Labour's devolution is
finally implemented it will inexorably bring with it the clarities
and rigidities which go with written constitutions, as well as the
basis of a constitutional court.

Hailsham and Scarman both want to see the political process
brought within the jurisdiction of the courts; and both appear
to share a preference for using the existing system rather than
creating a separate set of constitutional courts. Scarman in
particular wants to preserve the traditional unity of the law,
which has anyway been fragmented by the introduction of so
many tribunals. They are right in this. The experience of the
Industrial Relations Court served as a warning against further
proliferation and division of judicial or quasi-judicial processes.
At the same time, it is doubtful whether the rather haphazard
composition of the Judicial Committee—made up of senior
British judges, some Commonwealth judges and certain British

Privy Councillors—would really prove acceptable for very long. The Commonwealth judges admittedly may lend both relevant experience and distinction; but with time the Judicial Committee is likely to lose its jurisdiction outside the UK, and the case for merger with the House of Lords will become stronger. It should be remembered, of course, that there are representatives of Scottish as well as English law among the Law Lords.

It also seems desirable to accept the recent willingness of judges, particularly in the Court of Appeal, to overrule ministers in the exercise of their executive powers if the courts feel that these powers are being misused, as in the Tameside case. This is to accept the common law tradition that statute should not be the sole determination of our laws and liberties: there is still room for custom, equity, and common sense.

The courts, however, cannot do much more than limit abuses from the executive or occasionally from over-mighty subjects: if a real restraint is needed on the power of the Commons we must look at other devices. These might include proportional representation, the referendum, a degree of entrenchment on constitutional laws, and a reformed second chamber.

Proportional representation is not, of course, a way of altering the power of the Commons as a whole: it is rather seen as a restraint on the dominance of a minority party. That there is a case for it in equity can hardly be disputed: the national tally of seats certainly does not represent the national tally of votes. Moreover, PR would clearly tend to produce coalition politics with the centre party or parties often having a place in government, or at least a say in its formation. This has understandable appeal; I myself would have welcomed experience of proportional representation through the European Assembly and the Scottish and Welsh Assemblies (if they are to come about). But I have important doubts about PR for Westminster.

For one thing, in its pure single transferable vote (STV) form it represents the end of the constituency system as we have known it—the end of a relationship marked by many ups and downs, but which can be immensely enriching and stimulating to MPs and of true value to the interests of their constituents. STV means much bigger units with groups of MPs; and we should have learned by now that bigger units are not necessarily better. Moreover, under STV the selection of representatives would tend to be less locally based and controlled more firmly by the central parties.

Perhaps it would be worth losing these things *if* we could gain more stable and effective government as a result. Whether we would must be a matter of argument. The American first-past-the-post two-party system is very stable; a growth in the number of significant parties, which PR may bring about, does not necessarily make for stability. It would be likely to enhance compromise and consent; but bold individualism based on firm convictions is also important, and that may suffer. I doubt that PR would do all that it is claimed for it by its advocates, and I believe that governments elected under our traditional system should normally try to operate through the consent which PR is designed to bring about. However, if PR is to come, I can see it working only in some form of the German additional member system, which adds proportionally-elected members to the traditionally-elected constituency members.

What of the current discussion of restraints on the power of the Commons? As I have argued already, an over-mighty Commons is not our greatest problem. Certainly I doubt whether many of its members feel a great sense of power; those in government are likely to be as conscious of the limitations as the strength of their power. Nevertheless, the power of the Commons alone to make any constitutional change it wishes, with only a minimum of restraint from the House of Lords, *is* excessive as the law now stand; and it is not satisfactory that our present second chamber has to be so circumspect in the use of its powers.

Oddly enough, the one balance to the power of the Commons that has made headway—the referendum—has done so not because of any conscious attempt to find a counter-weight to that power, but because of party manouvering and lack of confidence among Members of Parliament. Both the EEC and the two devolution referenda were brought about largely for internal Labour party reasons; while the devolution referenda also reflected a reluctance on the part of MPs who supported them to take responsibility for killing the devolution Bills. Labour opponents of devolution hoped that the referenda would apply the quietus which they themselves had not the nerve to apply.

Referenda could be used for three types of decisions: decisions about sovereignty, those on other constitutional matters, and decisions on issues of popular interest. The Northern Ireland Border Poll is an example of the first: the devolution referenda (because they do not consider the possibility of independence) of the second; and a poll on capital punishment would be an example of the third. The EEC referendum might be said to be a blend of the first and second.

It is easy to see why the case for referenda is attractive: they are in an obvious sense democratic, their results should command consent, and they are capable of providing at least some form of counterweight to the so-called 'elective dictatorship', with its ability to effect drastic and arbitrary change.

The case was considered in a careful report on 'The Referendum and the Constitution' (Old Queen Street Paper, Conservative Research Department, September 1978) produced by a committee under the chairmanship of Mr Nicholas Edwards MP. The committee came to the view that it is as a constitutional safeguard that the referendum is most urgently needed and most easily reconciled with our existing system. But the report recognized some of the powerful objections to referenda: the way in which they have been used by authoritarian governments and demagogues and their vulnerability to abuse; the way that they can be used to block desirable change; the difficulty of drafting fair questions; the risk that complex questions may be much over-simplified or misunderstood; the particular difficulty of deciding how a referendum should be triggered off; the advantage that lies with governments if they control the timing of referenda; and above all the problem of how to reconcile the referendum with our traditional concept of representative parliamentary democracy. Should referenda be binding or consultative? If they are consultative will they force a wedge between electorate and members who do not accept the popular verdict?

These are formidable objections, and they are made more powerful by the fact that the introduction of the referendum seems to reflect a loss of confidence in our system and our governors—a loss of confidence which in turn may further weaken our system. Moreover, for the 'elective dictatorship' we may substitute the dictatorship of a majority that does not have to consider the position of minorities, as the House of Commons should.

What, then, are we to make of these broad forms of referendum? Clearly, the general referendum (on other than constitutional or sovereignty questions) has the least to be said for it; I do not think we should make provision for it.

The sovereignty case is stronger, though there may be considerable difficulty in deciding on the relevant electorate. For example, the Northern Ireland Border Poll was criticized because its electorate was confined to the six Counties. Was Sudetenland a valid area in the days of the pre-War Czech crisis? This is a real point, which cannot be answered by rule of thumb. Nevertheless, it is reasonable to put to the people of Ulster (or for that matter of Scotland or Wales) the question of which country they wish to belong to, and insist that the results of such a referendum should be binding.

But what about the constitutional referendum? The Edwards Committee argued for a Constitution (Fundamental Provisions) Bill which would provide for a referendum before any change in the Constitution occurs. The Bill would ensure in particular that the existence of the Second Chamber was guaranteed, unless a referendum determined otherwise. (The power of the Commons ultimately to decide this matter on its own, brought in in 1911, would disappear). The Bill might also provide for referenda on proposed changes to the unity of the realm, the position of the Crown, the Bill of Rights and the system of election to the House of Commons. A commission would be set up to supervise referenda and draft the questions.

These proposals are worth considering very carefully. The Commons can too easily use a very narrow majority (based on a minority of the voting electorate) to throw into oblivion a Chamber that has existed for hundreds of years. Yet if we believe in the Parliamentary system we should not be afraid to let it tackle such profound questions as this. Perhaps a better answer is to provide that a fundamental change to the House of Lords, if resisted by that House, could be implemented only if it were deferred and re-enacted after the subsequent general election. The same would apply to other constitutional changes. This seems the best practical way of arriving at a limited degree of entrenchment, without the total upheaval of a full-scale written constitution.

Major constitutional reform is most justifiable in the House of

Lords. The matter has come to the fore not only through attacks from the Left, led by Michael Foot, but also with the notable speech by Lord Carrington, himself a hereditary peer, at the 1976 Tory Party Conference, when he called for an elected chamber, and the report by the Committee set up by Mrs Thatcher under Lord Home. ('The House of Lords', Conservative Central Office, March 1978.)

Calls for the reform of that ancient chamber are no new thing. Before 1914 it was of course a burning issue. Since 1945 the Lord's delaying power has been reduced and life peerages introduced. Labour tried in the 1960s (with Conservative support) to change the basis of the Lords' membership—though that effort ran aground, thanks to the famous Foot/Powell axis. Labour peers, led by Lord Champion, have recently had their say. And all the time there has been steady sniping from those on the Left who believe that the Lords should be abolished and that the country should switch to unicameral government. Indeed the 1977 Labour Party conference passed a motion to this effect.

The debate rumbles on. It was given new life when the Labour government rammed through Parliament a succession of thoroughly socialist measures, disregarding the low proportion of the electorate which had voted Labour at the general election. Doubtless they were legally entitled to behave in this way, but then equally the House of Lords was entitled to resist this legislation to the extent of invoking the delaying power. Events showed clearly that however much the Lords might reflect popular feeling on much of the legislation concerned, the basis of the Lords composition inhibited their powers. Their moral legitimacy in obstructing the will of the Commons is circumscribed.

Inevitably, therefore, thought has turned to ways of giving them that legitimacy: the authority to use the powers that legally they possess. It is true that they used their powers on the Aircraft and Shipbuilding Bill, the Dockwork Regulation Bill and over Felixstowe Docks, but it is most unsatisfactory for the House of Lords to have to assess whether it is expedient that they use the powers which Parliament as a whole has granted them, and a system of checks and balances which depends so heavily on delicate tactical judgements must risk ineffectuality.

What is the case for a second chamber? It is summed up in the Inter-Parliamentary Union's compendium *Parliaments of the World* (1976):

> At present, the bicameral system can no longer be explained by the need for a separate aristocratic representation. It justifies itself by two arguments:
> —in federal states, the bicameralism reflects the dualist structure of the state;
> —in unitary states, the adoption of bicameralism reflects the desire, either to have within the parliamentary machine an in-built mechanism, in the form of a so-called 'revising' chamber, to maintain a careful check on the sometimes hasty decisions of a first Chamber, or, to achieve a more stable balance between the Legislature and the Executive as the unbridled power of a single Chamber is likely to be restrained by the creation of a second Chamber on a different basis.

In Britain we are still talking about a unitary state (in spite of the attempt of the Liberals to promote federalism), and it is therefore the second argument that concerns us here. That in turn breaks down into two elements, though they are not, as the IPU seems to imply, mutually exclusive.

The first of these, the revising function, is the less controversial. Even Labour ministers who huff and puff about the Lords do not seem to mind too much their additional scrutiny of, and opportunity to amend, legislation provided; nor do they reject the chance of initiating some of their flood of Bills in the upper house. Presumably they would say that if the Lords were abolished the Commons would find ways of giving still more time and thought to Bills; but it is hard to see where if would come from, without further over-burdening the timetable.

But it is the second argument that is the heart of the matter. John Stuart Mill expressed it trenchantly:

> a majority in a single assembly . . . easily becomes despotic and overweening if released from the necessity of considering whether its acts will be concurred in by another constituted authority. The same reason which induced the Romans to have two consuls makes it desirable there should be two chambers; that neither of them may be exposed to the corrupting influence of undivided power, even for the space of a single year.

There are, of course, other arguments for a second chamber in a unitary state. It can, for example, involve in the business of government people who may not be available for the often more time-consuming work of the first chamber. It can give a chance for a variety of interests to be represented, either formally or informally (depending on its composition). But the essence is the power to force re-thinking and to delay. The charges that a second chamber adds to the burden of the government, may be filled with nonentities, is prone to conservatism and can thwart the will of the people have to be measured against these benefits.

How have other countries resolved this question? According to the IPU booklet, thirty out of forty-two unitary states studied, but none of the fourteen federal state, have adopted a uni-cameral legislature. Among the unitary states, however, a number are small, and the unitary socialist countries tend to be impatient of the delays and trouble caused by having two chambers (one is probably bad enough!). In the end, foreign experience is of somewhat limited value; one has to decide according to what suits this country.

When we talk of the need to restrain government, obviously Tories think of the kinds of measures that flooded the Statute Book and the Parliamentary timetable during the first two years of the 1974 Labour government: the Aircraft and Shipbuilding Bill, the Community Land Act, the 1974 Rent Act, the attack on pay-beds, the statutory imposition of comprehensive secondary education, and some of the Chancellor's tax policies. These were generally unpopular measures; in addition several of them were riddled with practical defects. They were often quite simply bad legislation.

Clearly, however, we cannot base our case solely on socialist measures. The job of an effective second chamber would be to hold up or force reconsideration of questionable legislation from any source. Looking back on the 1970–4 Tory government, it may be argued that there were ingredients, at least, in its reforms of industrial relations, local government, housing finance, and the National Health Service which were not satis-factory. Views will vary about these matters, but it is at least possible that an effective second chamber could have led to more successful legislation, because it would have provided a sort of second opinion and because it would probably tend to support policies which were reasonably widely acceptable and which had a chance of surviving successive changes of government. No one can be sure that this is what would happen, but the expectation and intention would be that a second chamber's foot would turn more readily to the brake than to the accelerator.

What of the second chamber's composition and its powers? Logic suggests that we should look at the latter first, though the two are interrelated.

It is tempting to dream up a variety of new or extended tasks for our second chamber. In particular, there is the view that it should become much more representative of specific interest groups (a view that we shall consider when we look at its composition). Alternatively, it could be recast to represent the regions of the country, in the manner of second chambers in federal states like West Germany or the USA. But this presupposes that we are to become a regionalized nation, which is not—I hope—the case. In fact the best way of bringing about a more effective second chamber is for there to be virtually no change in its powers at all.

For the problem again is not so much that the Lords lack powers as that they lack the conviction in their right to use them to the full. Neither inheritance nor appointment gives the legitimacy that is seen today to lie in election on a universal suffrage.

This view is disputed by some. They argue that the present House of Lords is well-respected by the country, that custom and tradition give it ample legitimacy, and that constitutional engineering is a hazardous and unwanted activity. They may be right: elective democracy *may* not be as popular as is assumed. But all I can say is that the balance of the argument seems to point the other way and that experience in recent years does not suggest that the Lords have been able to restrain governments from perpetuating bad and unpopular measures.

The Home Committee, in its report on 'The House of Lords', argued that in spite of the case for an all-elected chamber, the best hope of constructive reform lies with a combination of election and nomination: 'application of the principle of election would ensure that it represented in some degree the spread of party opinion in the country; application of the nomination principle would allow some historic continuity with the House of Lords as presently constituted to be preserved' (pages 22–23). The assumption was that out of a total membership of 400, at least sixty per cent would be elected. The remainder (up to 160) would initially be recruited from the present House of Lords, with subsequent appointments being made by the Prime Minister, aided by the advice of a committee of Privy Councillors.

The Home Committee's report argues that this mixed membership would not only have the merit of greater continuity than the fully elected chamber, but would also allow elder politicians and eminent people from fields other than politics to continue to serve in the legislature. They believe that a fully elected second chamber would be more likely to challenge the Commons, with deadlock resulting. These arguments are no doubt true; but against them is the fact that today only election secures legitimacy, and that if we want a stronger second chamber we have to face the risk of great conflict—though, as we shall see, it is necessary for one or the other of the houses to be ultimately supreme. The Home Committttee evidently feel that their scheme would be more generally acceptable; no one can be sure, but I believe that a chamber that is fully elected is more likely to reach the Statute Book.

There is also, of course, a case for extending the second chamber's delaying power from one year to two, or alternatively to a new Parliament. The first idea looks attractive in theory, and should be our target. (I have already discussed special provisions for constitutional legislation.) But against this there is fact that constitutional reform should command as much all-party consent as is feasible. While an *extension* of the powers of the second chamber might be strongly resisted, it would be harder to oppose the case for merely converting an undemocratic chamber into a democratic chamber.

For the same reason, I would not contemplate giving the second chamber powers over money. Indeed, it is fairly common in other countries to confine the power of supply to the lower chamber and this has often been true over the long history of our own country.

It may be said that a second chamber that had little or no more power than the present House of Lords would not in fact make much difference. But it is important to realize that the Lords could not only use their delaying power with easier minds —they would in fact be able to use the traditional right of parliamentarians to spin out legislation and harass government: they would not be so subject to moral blackmail 'Hurry up, the People are waiting for this'.

I do not, then, believe the primary necessity to be in the overt relationship between the two houses, but rather to be the composition of the upper house. How should it be made up? So far I have argued that to provide the necessary authority the basis of membership must be democratic election. Should this be true of every member?

For a start, the bishops and the Law Lords, both groups traditional life peers, do not clearly *have* to be in the Lords; but probably they should be. The same perhaps applies to certain members of the royal family. But beyond that, every member should be elected—and elected on universal suffrage. Specifically, I reject the notion of direct representation of interest groups—whether trade unions, management, consumers, farmers, learned professionals, or anyone else. This also applies to peers, who would however be entitled to keep their titles and to the ordinary right to vote and stand for Parliament.

There is the school of thought which backs the creation of either an industrial parliament or at least a strong element of industrial representation in the second chamber. The basis of the argument is that great power lies in industry and it is much better therefore to involve the leaders of industry (notably in the unions) in the business of government than to leave them as a potentially disruptive force outside. The point is made that historically Parliament has always represented the power blocs. The barons in the Middle Ages, the great landowners in the period analysed by Namier were a part of the parliamentary system, which was able to mediate between the groups and moderate their power.

As we have seen already the idea has been tossed around in various forms, and various countries. Both Churchill and Leo Amery espoused it at points in their careers. The Weimar Republic and postwar France have both had shots at it; and one can even see traces in it in the ideas put forward for the televised NEDC as a forum for determining national economic policy. But this sort of approach has gained most acceptance in those described as corporatist.

The fact that corporatism has been allied with fascism should not mean that we should automatically rule out any notion of industrial representation—any more than should the fact that corporatism has grown more naturally in the more collectivist traditions of Catholicism than among the more individualistic Protestants. Nevertheless, we must consider the acceptability of picking out certain groups in society and formally conferring additional power on them: it certainly seems to conflict with the notion of one man, one vote.

Some of those who have argued most powerfully for an element of industrial representation in the second chamber—for example the late John Mackintosh in the PEP Broadsheet *Reshaping Britain*—have of course done so in the context of a second chamber that was clearly subordinate to the Commons: they have said that industry should have a chance to represent its views and even seek agreement in some sort of parliamentary framework; but that whatever it did would ultimately be subject to the approval of disapproval or the truly democratic body. Certainly if we were to have some sort of industrial parliament this should be the case. But in fact I prefer another approach.

This would be to make it possible for the leaders of industry —and of other fields—to sit in the second chamber, provided that they were willing to stand for election by all the people. It would be all to the good if this led to the membership of important men and women in the unions, the CBI, and anywhere else in Parliament—as the union leaders indeed often were fifty years ago. For this reason, among others, it would *not* be the intention that membership of the upper house should be anything like a full-time job (nor should it be paid on more than a modest basis). The tendency of all bodies to take on more and more work would have to be firmly resisted—and so far as possible pairing liberally operated!

If the essence of the second chamber is to be democratic election, what should be the voting system and the frequency of elections? There could be two categories of elected membership. The first of these would be the eighty-one UK members of the European Assembly. It is widely accepted that dual membership of the House of Commons and the Assembly imposes a strain;

at the same time, the fear that the two bodies will grow further and further apart is a real one and the possibilities of friction between the two bodies are serious. Membership of all the Assemblymen in the second chamber could do a good deal to alleviate this. However, this proposal is one that needs particularly careful discussion, and is not essential to my approach. The Home Committee rejected it, on the grounds that the Assemblyman would be elected for a quite different purpose and would anyway be heavily engaged in Europe.

The second category of membership, the ordinary members, would be elected on a different basis from that of the Commons, and would thus provide a balance to it. Another of the objectives of the whole reform is to secure a greater stability of policy. This suggests fixed-term elections, on a rotating basis. The American Senate pattern of six-yearly terms, with a third of the membership coming up for election every two years, looks appropriate.

It might also be appropriate to introduce some form of proportional representation. Again, since the object was to produce a counter-balance to the Commons, PR for the Commons would by no means inevitably follow. How this would work would be a matter needing detailed discussion. One possibility would be to use whatever system was finally selected for the European Assembly; another is perhaps the single transferable vote on a county or Euro-constituency basis. The fear that we are becoming swamped with elections is one that would have to be considered: it might therefore be desirable to combine the second chamber elections with the European elections—though this would mean a different pattern from the American Senate system.

How large should the second chamber be? This is a matter of judgement; but it seems reasonable to think of the eighty-one European Assemblymen constituting about a quarter of the second chamber. Certainly the aim should be a body appreciably smaller than the House of Commons and very much smaller than the present full membership of the House of Lords.

There is a view that an elected second chamber of the kind postulated here might even acquire a greater authority in the country than the House of Commons; and if it were based on proportional representation it could be held to be more truly representative than the first-past-the-post Commons. It is also argued that the history of the American Senate shows how an upper house can accumulate more power than was intended when it was set up.

I doubt, however, that this would happen in a body which did not grant supply, was less well paid than the Commons, and whose powers were clearly more limited than those of the Lower House. It would certainly not be the intention that the second chamber should overshadow the Commons—though with an evolutionary constitutional tradition like ours one can never be absolutely certain what may happen.

Ideally, constitutional reform should never be rushed: indeed, it may be that the scheme put forward here should incorporate specific additional hurdles for constitutional matters (for example, agreement between houses or additional delaying powers). Perhaps too it would be wiser to treat decisions on a second chamber in conjunction with other issues like devolution, electoral reform and a Bill of Rights. Yet the *prima facie* case for reform of the second chamber is strong, and it would be wrong to allow it to disappear in a vast swamp of controversy.

Let me sum up. I do not go so far as Lord Hailsham: I do not see an over-mighty Commons as the great problem. We should approach constitutional reform cautiously and with as much bipartisan agreement as possible. Nevertheless, there are substantial changes that should come about to provide some restraint on the power of the House of Commons and to help preserve those higher liberties and rights that may now be imperilled.

A written constitution is likely to emerge only very gradually. Membership of the EEC and devolution to Scotland and Wales (if they come) are of course steps in that direction, and the incorporation of the European Convention of Human Rights in our domestic legislation in some shape or form would be a further step. But the possibility of achieving enough agreement to bring in a whole new dispensation looks remote. Agreement is a long way off on proportional representation, anyway for the Commons—and their hostility is more than a simple matter of seeking to preserve their own seats.

The referendum as a vehicle for settling matters other than

those in which sovereignty is at stake has grave defects. Devolution may help, but only if we come up with a sensible scheme (something I discuss in Chapter 6). A judiciary prepared to stand up to the Executive and to uphold our traditions of freedom is also desirable; and of course the transfer of some powers to Europe and devolution make a degree of judicial review almost inescapable. But the change which to me offers most scope for an improvement in our allocation of political power is the strengthening of the second chamber. It keeps the additional checks and balances that we need within the realm of elected politics; it is democratic without being populist; and it does not entail upheaval to bring it about. There will, of course, be a major job of persuasion (among all parties) if it is to come about. It is on that, in my view, that reformers should concentrate.

5

An Effective Parliament

At the heart of my argument is the idea that instead of dispersing political power through referenda or various forms of corporatism we should continue to concentrate it in Parliament (and its complement, the law). Moreover, although the second chamber should be reformed and strengthened, ultimate political sovereignty should still lie with the House of Commons. The Commons will continue to play the major part in the making of our laws, the provision of the executive, the scrutiny of that executive, and the expression of the views and interests of the people that it represents, as well as the safeguarding the people's liberties.

This is a formidable list of tasks, and they are clearly not being done to popular satisfaction. Part of the trouble may be that the public see the powers of Parliament as wider than they are, including, for example, the ability to transform deep-grained cultural attitudes to work. But it is in the nature of our condition that politicians cannot shrug their shoulders and say 'don't blame us'. The tentacles of government nowadays spread so wide that politicians *will* be blamed—and politicians may have brought that blame upon themselves.

There are many criticisms of our system of Parliamentary government, but probably the fundamental one is that it has not proved capable of handling economic and industrial policy in our modern society. One hears it said that Parliament is perfectly capable of dealing with individual rights and perhaps even with social policy; but that it cannot cope with matters like unemployment, inflation, incomes policy, productivity, industrial relations, and the modernization of industry generally. Criticism of the present system has intensified over the last few years, fuelled by our poor economic performance.

63

First, the adversarial nature of Parliamentary politics has made for constant chopping and changing of policy as governments come and go. Parliament operates on a short life cycle, but industry must think in the medium and long term. Nationalization and denationalization, swings in regional policy, the tergiversations on incomes policy, and the repeated changes in the institutions which monitor it, the constant switches on industrial relations, land policy, and taxation—all are examples of the difficulties created for industry by our party system and the lack of consensus.

Coupled with this is our tendency to produce too much legislation without weighing the cost of legislation to those who have to implement it. Indeed, some of our recent employment protection legislation may actually have added to unemployment because it has made the costs of employing people too high.

Third, the debate in Parliament on economic matters may often be amateurish, unpredictable, and excessively partisan. Too few members have real knowledge of industry and finance. The major producer interests, management, and unions, are inadequately represented in Parliament.

Fourth, the system has proved particularly weak in its handling of the nationalized industries. Commitments to allow them to be run as ordinary industrial concerns have been repeatedly up-ended for short-term political reasons. The prices charged and decisions about investment and the location and closure of plants have been particularly affected.

Fifth, Parliament's relations with outside bodies seem confused. I have in mind the weakness of its links with NEDC and the uncertainty about the powers of Select Committees in relation to the bodies they examine and the witnesses and evidence they call.

Sixth, members are sometimes limited by the horizons of their constituencies; sometimes they do not look effectively at broader economic factors, particularly international ones.

This adds up to an indictment that cannot be ducked by supporters of traditional parliamentary democracy like myself. I aim to consider how we should respond to the challenge and whether there are ways in which Parliamentary government could become more effective, particularly in the economic sphere.

Let us consider first the six criticisms I have outlined.

In many ways the first is the crucial objection. The party battles, the marching and counter-marching, have produced an unstable climate for industry in recent years and it is not surprising that people have become interested both in taking the economic battle out of Parliament and in electoral reform as a means of achieving coalition governments of the centre. It may be that electoral reform would help to produce greater stability, as it appears to have done in Germany. However, the adversary system also serves as a way of acting out class and political struggles; it gives those with more extreme views at least the possibility of progress through peaceful political action. Consensus or coalition politics could drive the left and right further to the extremes.

Even-so, it is difficult to avoid the conclusion that adversary politics have become too dominant and destructive, and thus often out of tune with the wishes of the electorate. This tendency probably owes a good deal to the rise of the Left in the Labour Party, and the reactions to it. Labour leaders, notably both Sir Harold Wilson and Mr Callaghan, often seem to feel that in order to pacify the Left they must adopt an exaggerated aggressive attitude towards the opposition. Conservatives naturally respond aggressively. The party battle is nothing new, but it seems to have been sharpened by class-based politics. Many MPs on both sides of the House are unhappy about this. Some despair of altering the characteristics of the Chamber of the House of Commons and look to the development of committees as a way of reducing unnecessary conflict. There is something in this, but governments could wisely work harder within the Chamber to achieve agreement where possible, rather than merely trying to win battles. The 1971 Industrial Relations Act might well have survived if there had been rather more accommodation by the government of the day; moreover, if concessions had been made within the House of Commons the disastrous outside opposition might have been countered.

It is, moreover, an error to emphasize altering institutions rather than altering attitudes. With government leadership, however, changes in attitude are possible. Parliament may be seen as a constructive, if argumentative, national forum as well as a battleground.

This matter of leadership also applies to the over-production of legislation. In 1974–6, the Labour government pushed through a spate of measures on trades unions, shipbuilding and aircraft nationalization, employment protection, community land, pay beds, comprehensive education, dockwork regulation, tired cottages, and other matters. This experience has been widely seen as the promotion of unpopular legislation and a gross overloading of the law-making system. This made proper consideration of much of the legislation impossible, not least because the programme could only be rammed through with the aid of extensive guillotining. In the 1977–8 session, the decision to run three constitutional measures, on Scottish and Welsh devolution and on European elections made guillotining inevitable, and adequate discussion of the Scotland Bill impossible.

The problem is not just that inadequate discussion leads to worse legislation. There is also simply more legislation than industry, in particular, can digest. Energy which should be directed toward making and selling has to be diverted to form-filling and wrangling with government departments. But it is not only industry that suffers; local government is also afflicted in the same way by measures such as the ineffective Community Land Act, or the complications imposed by the legislation on homelessness and tied cottages. Neither measure added to the housing stock and in the latter case it may serve to reduce it in years to come. (Similarly, the effects of pay bed legislation are to damage the National Health Service, rather than private medicine.) The only answer to all this is, quite simply, to legislate less. This will not necessarily come about by institutional changes, but by the will of governments though Committee changes could have their effect on the flow of new laws.

What about the capacity of Parliament to debate economic and industrial policy effectively, given both its composition and its procedures?

Clearly neither top industrialists nor top trades unionists are likely to be members; they have not got the time, or in many cases the desire. Managers-turned-politicians are likely to find it hard to reconcile themselves to the fact that the majority of members have no executive role. Trades union leaders are normally brought up in a more political climate, where

argument and persuasion play a large part, but they may understandably feel that their impact and power are greater in
industry than they would be in Parliament.

But is it a serious weakness not to include many industrialists?
I doubt whether overall it is. For one thing, although the top
men from industry may not be in the House, there are a considerable number who have come in from business, or the union
movement, many of whom keep up active contacts there, and
who may have political talents which more senior men in
industry do not possess. Manufacturing industries are less well
represented than finance on the Conservative side, which is a
pity; but it is important to appreciate that the job of MPs is not
to negotiate, or even act as brokers between conflicting factions
and interests, but to understand, question, and where necessary
legislate. If a second chamber, reformed on the lines I have
discussed in Chapter 4, can attract industrial members, well and
good. But I do not accept the idea of a specifically industrial
Parliament, or a Parliament of the interests or corporations.

I must reiterate that the idea of institutionalizing the power of
the producers in society, by giving them a special place in the
constitution, is alien to the principles of liberal democracy.
There is no moral ground for over-ruling the principles of one
man, one vote, and of the equality between electors, by granting
a privileged position to those who happen to be at work in
certain occupations. Nor would an industrial Parliament necessarily be less adversarial than the present House of Commons;
it might provide an additional well-publicized forum for the
industrial differences. The notion that it could be a vehicle for
mediation and negotiation between the two sides of industry is
also questionable: a Parliament is not a negotiating body in
that sense. If that sort of negotiation is thought desirable,
NEDC exists as a vehicle for it.

It may be that what is envisaged is not a body with the
powers of decision that mark a Parliament, but an assembly that
would make recommendations to the existing Parliament and
provide a knowledgeable analysis of legislation and economic
and industrial policy generally. This could be expressed in its
general debates, and in the work of committees dealing with
investigation and legislation.

There is a stronger case here. Even so, one may doubt whether

members of such a body would have the sort of all-round expertise which this approach implies, or the time to exercise it in
conjunction with their normal work. It looks more fruitful to
seek out ways of making sure that expertise is available to the
present Parliament.

Underlying the notion of a House of Industry, however, is the
belief that industry's representatives would be bound into policies they had had a larger part, in shaping, and would behave
more 'responsibly' as a result. If incomes policy was of their
own making, they would operate it more effectively. This was,
indeed, to some extent the rationale behind the Social Contract:
the barons would be brought into the fold. But I think this is
questionable. And might it not even follow that their rank and
file would be increasingly susceptible to extreme, maverick
leadership with a dangerous tipping of power towards the
militants? The strain on the trades union movement could be
very considerable.

The next criticism of the present system is that both Parliament and government have proved peculiarly inept in the handling of the nationalized industries. It is difficult to rebut this:
short-term policy objectives of the industries, and in some cases
threats of nationalization and/or denationalization have made
long-term planning and development almost impossible. The
desire to provide or maintain jobs (and sometimes to win or
hold Parliamentary seats) has made improved productivity hard
to come by.

The history of the steel industry provides a paradigm of this,
as was illustrated in a penetrating article in *The Listener* ('Hoops
of Steel', 26 January 1978) by Sir Ieuan Maddock, a former chief
scientist to the Department of Trade and Industry. He attacked
not only the changes in steel policy since the War, but also the
superficiality and indeed, as he sees it, irresponsibility of the
Select Committee on Nationalized Industries' approach to
British Steel:

> The more that industry and commerce come under the yoke of
> Parliament, the more vital it is that Parliament should be con-
> cerned with stable and wise long-term policies and leave it to the
> appropriate organisations to get on with the job of implementing
> such plans ... let the Select Committees, at all times, remind
> the House that, whatever the apparent advantages of this policy,

or that dogma, the price of constant change and constant interference is inefficiency, demoralisation and, ultimately, complete
surrender to our international competitors.

This is only one aspect of the problem of the political handling
of the nationalized industries; it is hardly necessary to detail
others, such as the ministerial interference in pricing and investment. It is tempting to say that the only way out is not to
nationalize; but that will not quite do, partly because it ignores
the existence of industries which clearly are not going to be
denationalized in any forseeable circumstances, and partly
because it leads to the condition which Sir Ieuan Maddock
analysed in the passage just quoted. No, the relationship must be
looked at more carefully.

So, too, must the relationship of Parliament with outside
bodies such as NEDC. The former Director-General of NEDC,
Sir Ronald McIntosh, has talked on a number of occasions
about the problem of linking his organization with Parliament.
In a symposium on *The Corporate State—Myth or Reality*
(Centre for Studies in Social Policy, pages 130–1) he was
reported as saying that our society is, and will remain, sufficiently complex to need some clearly identified interest groups
and some reasonably systematic arrangements for disciplining,
pre-digesting, and reconciling conflicts of interest. The need for
predigestion of this kind is greater in Britain than in many
other countries because of the peculiar nature of our adversary
political system in Parliament. McIntosh added that the problems of the relationship of NEDC with Parliament had baffled
him. He had yet to meet anyone within Parliament who had
the answer to it, and he believed that there is no effective way of
creating the link between the corporate aspects of our society
and Parliament until Parliament undertakes self-reform. In a
speech to the Bow Group on 31 March 1977, he said that what
he 'would most like to see is a decision by the appropriate
Select Committee or sub-committee to maintain a continuing
interest in and watch over the activities of NEDC and its
associated tripartite groups' (quoted Select Committee on
Procedure, 1977–8, Vol. III).

The sixth problem, that of the narrowness of view of Members
of Parliament, has a certain force. The House of Commons is

not, for the most part, a lofty senate; the blinkers of party and constituency are worn quite naturally for much of the time. Prejudice and ignorance exist, and debates may often seem excessively parochial as international problems like unemployment are reduced to constituency terms. The fact that those with constituency problems tend, understandably, to be chosen to speak in debates on subjects of this kind serves to reinforce the impression of narrowness. Yet there are compensations. MPs are not all wise statesmen, but they do roughly reflect the mood of the people they represent and there is an immediacy in the way in which the House works, a responsiveness to attitudes and developments outside, which may give too much dominance to the short-term view, but which has merits in maintaining some rapport between government and governed and in offsetting the isolation of bureaucracy. Still, too much of the Commons' debating time on important matters is directed to local newspaper headlines and too little to the heart of the matter.

What are we to make of all these criticisms? It is important, first of all, to understand that while Parliament *creates* the executive, it cannot *be* the executive. The formulation of policy and its execution must remain essentially with government, and government is entitled to try to carry out a coherent policy, not to be pushed to a series of ad hoc decisions. But governments must be able to persuade Parliament to support their policy. The rebuffs received by the recent minority Labour governments have been salutary, particularly where—as with the Devolution Bills—they have served to remind the government of the day that what it was seeking to do was not fundamentally supported by the House as a whole. It seems probable that the recent growth of voting independently of the Whips is likely to continue, particularly if the standing of the backbencher increases with better pay, greater resources, and the development of more effective roles in formulating policy and scrutinizing the Executive.

The occasional conflict between whips and backbenchers is part of the larger question of the balance between executive and legislature. The position of either can be pressed too far An extreme case for the primacy of government is to be found in the remarks of Lord Glenamara, formerly the Leader of the House,

Edward Short, quoted in the report of the Procedure Committee (p. viii). He considered that government must be able to 'secure from Parliament any necessary extension of their executive powers and to implement their election pledges, by legislation or otherwise' and that 'whatever changes we introduce should reinforce and not undermine effective Government'. The committee commented:

> We agree that the relationship between executive and legislature is the crucial feature of the functioning of our institutions of government, and we are conscious of the widespread concern in the country about the present nature of that relationship. But we do not believe that the criticisms will be answered, as Lord Glenamara's evidence suggested, merely by getting through the work demanded of the House by the Government more expeditiously and then by finding a 'worthwhile role' for the backbencher. The essence of the problem, as Lord Glenamara himself recognised, is that the balance of advantage between Parliament and Government in the day to day working of the Constitution is now weighted in favour of the Government to a degree which arouses widespread anxiety and is inimical to the proper working of our parliamentary democracy.

The Committee said that their aim was to enable

> the House as a whole to exercise effective control and stewardship over Ministers and the expanding bureaucracy of the modern state for which they are answerable, and to make the decisions of Parliament and Government more responsive to the wishes of the electorate.

They added that the task of Parliament falls into four main categories: legislation, the scrutiny of the activities of the Executive, the control of finance, and the redress of grievance.

This approach, like that of their report as a whole, was sensible. It is a pity that they did not have a chance to analyse what might be called a more enlightened variant of Lord Glenamara's view—that an increase in backbench power can make consistent overall policy harder to achieve and can over-emphasize short-term and immediately popular policy-making, at the expense of long-term coherence. In particular, it is difficult for government to pursue a steady financial strategy if bits and pieces of it are liable to abrupt alteration. But it is implicit in all that the Procedure Committee says that a more effective committee system would lead the backbenches to a fuller understanding of the strategic problems of government, including the need for continuity. What is certain is that ministers and officials will have to learn to argue their case harder and against more searching opposition as an informed committee structure develops, and that in itself must be good. Moreover, the notion propounded by Lord Glenamara—that the government is in some special sense the guardian of election pledges and therefore has a moral right to get its business regardless—is not compatible with carefully considered decision-making. The balance, therefore, needs to be tipped towards the House, provided that members see that more power means more responsibility.

Indeed we need generally to give more thought to the powers of ministers. It is all to the good that the courts should recently have been prepared to see that ministers do not act in breach of the law in matters like the Tameside and Laker cases. The scope for 'judge-made' law is obviously and rightly limited; but the scope for the executive and other powerful bodies acting within the traditions and principles of liberty and fairness that are embodied in the Common Law is not. Nobody should be too impressed by spurious sociological arguments about the upbringing of judges: their upbringing is in the Common Law of England, for which there need be no apology.

But the fact that judges may check ministers when they are in breach of the law is not the whole story. The time has come to consider the prerogative or non-statutory powers of ministers. Roughly speaking, it is held that ministers can do what they like provided that they do not breach the law, impose duties or liabilities on the subject and have the resources required for their actions. There is, in Sir Ivor Jenning's words, 'no general power to govern' (*Cabinet Government*, page 90); but equally there is no general limitation on government—which derives from the historical fact that our liberties have been wrested piecemeal from our rulers, rather than enshrined from the start in something like the United States Constitution.

These non-statutory powers were described by Mr Sam Silkin, speaking as Attorney-General in the House of Commons

(18 April 1978, (Volume 948, Column 408) as 'the sorts of powers which are exercised by Ministers of the Crown even if they step outside what is perhaps properly or constitutionally the subject of ministerial powers as such'. This may seem a curious phrase for the senior law officer to use; yet it embodies a reality. But if that is the reality, then it seems all the more important that the government of the day should operate within certain principles and conventions—for example, not 'legislating' by white paper and not seeking to implement its policies by selective inducements or arm-twisting. The recent Labour government repeatedly sought to make its incomes policies binding in ways that flouted these conventions. Thus the Remuneration, Charges, and Grants Act of 1975 incorporated a white paper (cmnd 6151) which could not be amended by Parliament and which included *as part of the law of the land* a statement by the TUC. In subsequent years, the government did not even present the exact terms of their incomes policy statements to the House for its formal approval. The enforcement of government decisions about pay limits through public sector contracts without those limits having even been put before Parliament was particularly objectionable. It may be 'legal', but it is alien to the spirit of the constitution. The true prerogative powers—notably over foreign affairs—are one thing: it is accepted that the powers once held by the monarch are now exercised by ministers. Other non-statutory powers, however, should be used with restrain. It is up to the back-benches to see that this happens.

There has been much talk in recent years about how backbenchers can be more effective. A reasonable level of pay and better office and research facilities and limited changes in the system could no doubt help; but I do not think that these rate very highly beside determination on the part of members to use the system that exists more effectively.

The backbencher who did most in the October 1974 Parliament to show the House what can be achieved by a resolute determination to use existing possibilities is unquestionably the Labour MP Mr George Cunningham. He has a shrewd eye for procedure, but fundamentally his achievements, whether on the devolution referendum 'threshold', pensions, or in other matters, have stemmed from a gritty determination to pursue the course he thinks right and to argue his case thoroughly. He has shown that backbenchers have considerable powers if they are prepared to use them.

Moreover, it is important to understand that the Chamber of the House of Commons is still of crucial significance in a number of ways. For a start, it is there that voting happens; whereas a government can duck any number of critical Select Committee reports, it cannot normally duck the consequences of a defeat in the lobbies, even though defeats have become rather more the order of the day recently, and rather less challenges to the whole viability of the government than used to be the case.

Almost equally important in the highly personalized world of politics is the fact that political reputations still depend to a very great extent on performance in the House. It might have been thought that the existence of television would have transformed this, but it has not. It plays a part in establishing reputations or weakening them, but effectiveness in the Commons is what really impresses other MPs, including the Whips, who have a considerable say in promotion and relegation.

Indeed it is arguable that the period of minority Labour government after 1974 has made the Chamber more important than it had been for years. I welcome this: instinctively I am on the side of those who wish to maintain the importance of the Chamber, both as forum and arbiter of events, and as a means of keeping pressure on the Executive. Moreover, I *like* the chamber—its human feeling, the drama, the rituals. Nevertheless, the criticisms of the Chamber must be taken very seriously. They fall into two categories: the frustrations imposed on members by the system, and, much more important, the damage done to continuity and rationality, particularly in economic and industrial policy, imposed by the adversary system. In a sense, both revolve round the point that, in Parliamentary politics, the destructive seems to be at a premium compared with the constructive. This is certainly the impression that listeners to the radio broadcasting of the House derive.

As I have said already, the flavour of the Commons will change only if members—and the Government in particular—wish it to change. But Governments, if they wish to change the climate, must seek to do so not at the point in the lifetime of a

Parliament when they are weakening, but at the moments when they are strongest. The conciliatory phase of recent governments has nearly always come when they have started to lose ground, and the other side is looking for the kill. It is hardly surprising that a government which spends its early days ramming through legislation in steam-roller style does not receive much sympathy when things become rougher for it. 'In victory, magnanimity' is not a bad motto in politics, as elsewhere.

Will broadcasting Parliament have a significant effect on its workings? I support broadcasting as a matter of principle: I believe that, so long as broadcasting does not produce a physical distortion of Parliament's proceedings, MPs do not have a right to prevent the public hearing and seeing what happens in their Parliament, any more than that in the past they were right to keep the press out. Sound radio has certainly had some effect on the way Parliament conducts itself: more members try to get in on Prime Minister's question time and both questions and answers seem rather more directed to the outside world than was formerly the case. The emphasis on the knockabout which already characterized the view of Parliament conveyed by some of the Parliamentary sketch writers has been reinforced by radio.

On the other hand, with time broadcasting should help the public have a fuller understanding of the processes of Parliament —perhaps to see why particular rituals have developed and even why sometimes barracking and noise have a certain justification, either as a way of expressing feelings which because of lack of time cannot be expressed more formally or as part of the process of making sure that ministers do not too easily get away with ill-thought positions. For a minister who does not bother to reply to a debate, but simply reads out a prepared brief, to be subjected to a certain amount of heckling is no bad thing; and a Parliament that was always on its best behaviour would risk dying on its feet.

It is unfortunate, nevertheless, that Prime Minister's questions should have become so much the staple of parliamentary broadcasting from its launching; and short of the ideal of a channel broadcasting the whole of Parliament's proceedings a better balance between rough and tumble and more measured debate has early proved necessary.

To achieve this should not be impossible, particularly if rather more broadcasting time could be made available. And if it can be achieved, then not merely will it be possible for the public to be better educated in the ways of Parliament, but also for Parliament to be more effective, whether consciously or unconsciously, in the education of the public in politics.

Overall, however, changes in the Chamber are likely to be of a somewhat intangible nature—a matter of attitudes as much as of procedure. But there is one area of Parliament where there is real scope for changes in procedure, and that is in the committee system. This has been the favourite stamping ground of academic would-be reformers of Parliament for many years, and no comparison can have been made more often than that between the effectiveness of committees in the American Congress and the British Parliament. But to some extent these discussions have missed the point. They have concentrated on the quality of committee enquiries and the back-up available to committees; but the crucial questions are to do with the *power* of committees and whether their views seriously influence events.

Certainly the reports of the Expenditure Committee or the Select Committee on Nationalized Industries may have some impact. Ministers and civil servants normally like the endorsement of a select committee report, and some reports receive good coverage in the media. Moreover, the Public Accounts Committee at least has always been treated with caution and respect by government departments. Yet at the end of the day, committee reports may vanish into thin air, often without even perfunctory debate in Parliament.

Does this matter? It does, for several reasons. For a start, the reports may in themselves be of considerable value. By and large they will be backed by substantial quantities of evidence, over which great trouble has been taken, and which is publicly available. The actual reports are naturally of variable quality. A certain amount will depend on who does the actual drafting—whether the committee clerk, a special adviser, the chairman, or a combination of these; and it may be said that reports are sometimes too laconic or under-argued. They may also be too heavily influenced by the fashionable notions of the day and sometimes lacking in intellectual rigour. Nevertheless, there are few reports which, with their oral and written evidence, are not worth thinking about carefully, and some are very much better than that—for example, some of those on public expenditure.

But it is not just that many reports are valuable documents: it is also true that the preparation of reports does a great deal to produce better Members of Parliament, who are able not only to hear authoritative evidence but also to have a glimpse into the policymaking process which is normally otherwise denied to backbenchers. Over the years committee members can build up valuable expertise in a field; and even those who say that it is the job of members to ask questions rather than provide answers will probably admit that, in some areas at least, expertise is the necessary prerequisite to penetrating questioning.

The question of how to make the best use of committees and of the expertise that they are capable of accumulating lay at the core of the very important *First Report from the Select Committee on Procedure Session 1977–1978* (published in August 1978), under the chairmanship of Sir Thomas Williams.

My own view of the problem has been that there is one major way of maximizing the value of committees; and this is to merge the select committees, which carry out investigations, with the standing committees, which deal with the committee stages of legislation. For standing committees *vote*, and in the Parliamentary system votes can outweigh any amount of discussion.

It follows, therefore, that the existing select committees—the Expenditure Committee, with its subject sub-committees, the Select Committees on Nationalized Industries, Race Relations, Overseas Aid, and so on—should be converted into subject committees, probably matching the existing government departments, and that they should undertake the tasks of conducting enquiries on the present lines, considering proposed legislation in White Paper or draft form, and handling the committee stages of legislation that are taken in standing committee. The aim would be to have continuity in the membership of these committees (rather than the system of ad hoc appointment which applies to standing committees); and the objective would be to build up groups of knowledgeable members who would base their positions on expertise as much as on fore-ordained party positions.

This is not to say that party should, or could, be eliminated from these committees. Because they would exercise a degree of real power, their composition should almost certainly reflect the party balance in the way that standing committees do; and it would be naive to suppose that the Whips could have no influence or that the members of the committees would become political eunuchs while they served on such committees. Yet continuing exposure to the problems of an area such as the steel industry, or housing and land, or pensions, could help to avoid the often damaging switching backwards and forwards of policy which has marked the post-war years.

Obviously these committees would not hold decisive power: that would still lie with Parliament as a whole, on the one hand, and with the government on the other. The decisions, votes or views of the new committees could be overturned, and the committees should not be in any way autonomous. Their power to send for persons and papers should continue to be exercised formally through the House—and the House must be willing to enforce it. Their task must be one of reporting to the House as a whole; but that at least could be put on a more effective basis than it is at present. It would be desirable to squeeze out of the parliamentary time-table one day a year for consideration of the reports of each committee, perhaps with a vote on whether or not to approve the report at the end of the day. But it would be in dealing with legislation that the new committees should really have an impact—an impact which might make life more difficult for the government's business managers, but which could lead to less ill-digested laws.

One question which has been argued is whether under a new committee structure the Public Accounts Committee and the Expenditure Committee should be merged. The leading advocate of this view is Mr Edward du Cann, who has himself been at different times Chairman of each of these Committees. His objective, as I understand it, is more effective financial scrutiny of government—a goal I share. But if the particular scrutinizing function of the PAC were merged with the broader policy analysis of the Expenditure Committee, an important discipline might be lost.

By and large, a single committee should cover the whole area of a particular department—otherwise the House would find itself with more committees than it could man. But there could be one or two exceptions. Separate committees for health and social security—two vast and largely separate areas—is one example. I would also favour two committees to cover the Treasury field, one dealing essentially with fiscal matters, and serving as the Committee on the Finance Bill, and the other concerned with economic and industrial strategy.

The idea of a total merger of select (or investigatory) and standing (or legislative) committees was one of those considered by the Select Committee on Procedure, as was the notion of re-casting select committees so that they matched government departments. The Select Committee adopted the latter approach, suggesting that there should be twelve committees. They would cover agriculture; defence; education, science, and arts; energy; environment; foreign affairs; home affairs; industry and employment; social services; trade and consumer affairs; transport; and Treasury. For the time being, these committees should be empowered to cover matters relating to Wales, Scotland, and Northern Ireland.

On the other hand, the Select Committee came down against the full merger of select and standing committees or the reference of the generality of Bills to select committees. Their arguments deserve to be read in full; but in essence they were as follows. First, select committees would lose their objectivity and freedom from party conflict. Second, the burden of legislative work would sometimes leave little or no time for their other functions: this has apparently happened in Ottawa, where this sort of system has been introduced. Third, it would be wrong to exclude from committee consideration of legislation a member who, although not on the committee, may have a real interest (including perhaps a constituency interest) in the subject. Fourth, the submission of Bills to the more informal procedures of select committees could produce acute problems of timing, which might make time-tabling inevitable.

Instead, therefore, the Committee put forward another approach designed to allow standing committees on certain Bills to begin their work on a Bill with an examination of its background and of relevant witnesses. This would take place (after a preliminary sitting) for up to three sittings of the committee. Committees which had this power would be known as public bill committees. Exactly which bills were subject to this procedure would be decided by the House, but the hope is that in time it would become the normal practice. It would also be the practice for some members of the select 'departmental' committees to serve on standing and public bill committees.

I myself still lean towards full integration of select and standing committees, since I believe that this would give the select committees a power that they will not otherwise acquire. I would be prepared to accept some loss of objectivity or non-partisanship in exchange. Nevertheless, the Select Committee's arguments obviously have considerable weight; and in the interests of making progress it would seem wise to support their implementation, and then see how matter develops.

Reform of the committee system could have an important impact on the effectiveness of Parliament; equally important is the need to improve Parliament's scrutiny and control of economic matters and of expenditure in particular. An economic and industrial strategy committee would be of particular importance, not so much because there would be much legislation going through it as because it would have the job of scrutinizing the government's public expenditure proposals (as the Expenditure Committee does at present) and also of serving as the Parliamentary link with NEDC and outside bodies concerned with such matters as the formulation of incomes policy. If trade union, CBI and other industrial leaders, as well as academics and other analysts, could discuss policy with such a committee, some of the fears of corporatism might be allayed and the argument for an industrial Parliament be reduced. Sir Ronald McIntosh himself made the same point (*The Times*, 1 April 1977), saying that he was 'most anxious that the work done by and under the aegis of NEDC should be ... clearly seen to be within the framework of our normal democratic processes' and that a link with Parliament would be welcome.

It might also be desirable for the government to present its whole economic, financial, and fiscal strategy in a revised form so that matching the fiscal strategy embodied in the Finance Bill there would be an economic statement covering public expenditure (presumably incorporating the essence of the present public expenditure White Paper) and the government's proposals for prices and incomes policy. This would be examined closely by the committee, which would also deal with the committee stage of any legislating (e.g. prices and incomes legislation) needed to put the policy into effect. Indeed, it is worth considering carefully whether we should not have a full-scale Expenditure Bill to match the Finance Bill.

Inherent in the idea of an economic and public expenditure statement is the notion that in some manner the House of Commons should set about regaining the control over supply that it has effectively relinquished in recent times—be it said, through its own decisions. Parliament seems to have become bored with examining supply in detail—and the so-called 'supply days' have of course become devoted to general debates, chosen for the most part by the Opposition.

It is interesting to see what has happened over time. In earlier years, the provision of supply was the main reason for summoning Parliament. The Committee of Supply appeared, along with the Committee of Ways and Means, in 1641. The main function of the former became approval of expenditure; of the latter the authorization of taxation. But the reformed nineteenth-century Parliaments became more interested in social reform and thus in spending money, and less in the examination of estimates. and by the mid-nineteenth century, supply debates seem to have become increasingly general in their subject matter. In 1896 Arthur Balfour introduced major reforms in the procedure, arguing in the process that

> while Supply does not exist for the purpose of enforcing economy on the Government, it does exist for the purpose of criticizing the policy of the Government, of controlling their administration, and bringing them to book for their policy at home and abroad. (H. C. Deb. 4th Ser. Vol. 37 col 272, 20.2 1896).

Twenty days were set aside for supply, and it became the practice for the Opposition to choose their subject matter. There have been changes in the procedure since, but supply days have remained essentially Opposition days—and the one thing Oppositions do not seem interested in discussing on them is supply.

That task was handed over to a committee—the Estimates Committee, which was set up in 1912

> To examine such of the Estimates presented to the House as may seem fit to the Committee, and to suggest the form in which

such estimates shall be presented for examination, and to report
what, if any, economies consistent with the policy implied in
those Estimates may be affected therein.

Until the 1939–45 war, they appear actually to have considered
the estimates, but after the war the lure of more general enquiries
proved too strong and the lack of expert backing too crippling.
They turned to more specific enquiries in particular areas by
small sub-committees. Later, however, a desire to delve more
deeply into the policies behind the estimates led to the replacement of the Estimates Committee by the Expenditure Committee, which was given the task of considering 'how, if at all, the
policies implied in the figures of expenditure and the estimates
may be carried out more economically', as well examining the
relevant papers. But once again the desire to be economical has
normally been submerged by other considerations, and a systematic examination of public expenditure has not emerged. As a
result, Parliament's control over expenditure has been nothing
like as tight as the control which the Finance Bill gives it in
respect of taxation. The introduction of cash limits and their
assimilation with the Estimates may have made tighter scrutiny
possible but there is a long way to go.

But that merely reinforces the point that if Parliament is to
have a more effective role in the handling of the economy, it
will have to accept a greater responsibility for what it does. Both
in the Chamber and in the committees, Parliament is often
slapdash and easy-going, as well as occasionally irresponsible.
Buggin's turn, a taste for agreeable jaunts, amateurishness, and
inconsistency can all be found occasionally in committee
behaviour, to the detriment of the reputation of the House as
well as the effectiveness of its work. It is as well to recognize
this. If we do not, we cannot claim the strengthened role that I
believe to be necessary if we are to preserve a free society of the
kind we have known, and avoid succumbing to corporatism or
collectivism in one or other of their guises.

This crucial Parliamentary task of sticking up for the individual could be implemented by transferring to direct Parliamentary control, via appropriate committees, of certain functions which at present come effectively within the government's
sphere. The Parliamentary Commissioner, or Ombudsman,

should clearly be the servant and appointee of the select committee which already exists to cover his activities. In addition, the National Consumer Council—if it is to continue to exist —should be appointed by Parliament rather than by government, and report back to Parliament. In neither case does this entail a loss of the true executive powers of government, which must be able to act firmly in its proper sphere.

6

De-Centralizing Government

Power must be assigned, where possible, in a clear-cut way to the appropriate democratically accountable body. The blurring of responsibility that characterizes state corporatism is damaging, and at all levels we need less but more effective government. In this chapter I shall apply this approach to what may be broadly called the central-local relationship. ('Local' covers not only local government but other services locally administered, such as health.)

London does not have a monopoly of widsom or virtue, and the greatness of the country will not be restored unless we can find ways of creating scope for those with vigour and imagination in *every* part of the country, rather than perpetuating the feeling that to get anywhere one has to come to London. By scope, I mean above all power—the possibility of taking important decisions which will affect the lives of one's fellow citizens. Local leaders must be more than agents of central government. Power must, where appropriate, be decentralized.

These words may seem odd coming from someone who has been an active Parliamentary opponent of the various devolution bills; but for reasons which I shall only summarize, these bills have not provided the right answer. In their different ways, the Scotland and Wales bills have been designed to split the national level of government, with some functions remaining in London but others going to Edinburgh and Cardiff. The result will be not only more government, but a diluting of central government. That would perhaps not matter if truly effective schemes of devolution could be devised; but the long debates showed that there are fundamental weaknesses in both Scottish and Welsh schemes. There is the now famous West Lothian problem—the fact that Scots MPs would be able to vote on English, Welsh, and Northern Irish education, health, housing, and so on, but not on those subjects in their own countries, while English, Welsh, and Northern Irish MPs would have no say on these subjects in Scotland. It adds up to an almost infallible recipe for friction; and while the Welsh equivalent problem would be less serious, because the Welsh Assembly would not be legislative, it will still be there. On top of this, there is in the Scottish case the very severe difficulty of separating economic from social policy, which is what the scheme basically is trying to do, as well as the considerable weakness which lies in a financial arrangement by which the Scottish Assembly would have to finance its work out of a block grant, with no safety device in the form of a local tax if over-spending—whether intentional or otherwise—should take place. In this the block grant is quite different from the Rate Support Grant of local government.

In the Welsh case, the peculiar difficulty seems to be the separation of the law-making function, retained by Parliament, from execution, given to the assembly. Moreover, even in execution it is only the statutory powers of Ministers, broadly speaking, that are transferred: the non-statutory, or prerogative, powers of Ministers generally remain with them—or disappear. At the same time, policy in Wales would be derived from two separate sources—the laws passed by Parliament and the desires of the assembly. The assembly would have no power to change those laws, except in relation to certain delegated legislation (itself a dubious concept); yet to say that in this respect it will simply be in the familiar position of local government is to miss the point. Perhaps the difference might be put like this: local government has to operate *under* the law, but the assembly will have to operate the law. The bulk of the role of the Secretary of State in relation to devolved matters will be transferred to the assembly. The split between legislation and implementation certainly runs counter to British political experience.

Devolution, then, in the Labour Government's approach, does not look viable; and the more logical alternative of federalism has a grave weakness in the UK context, where England so outweighs the other countries in size. But that does not mean that we should not seek or strengthen other forms of decentralization.

We have a long-established system of decentralization in local government; but in recent years its role and powers have become more and more uncertain. It has tended increasingly to become a tool of central government—indeed, it is arguable that state corporatism has gone further in local government than in industry. Local government has always been the creature of central government, in the sense that its existence is due to Acts of Parliament and that Parliament can always change those acts. In particular, local government has no powers other than those that Parliament is prepared to allow it. That is as it should be; but it does not follow that local government should exist to follow the central government's bidding.

What are the symptoms of this trend? They are too numerous to list in full, but I will pick out one or two important recent developments, drawing my examples from Conservative as well as Labour administrations.

One Conservative example was in Mr Peter Walker's Housing Finance Act, which created a national system for determining local authority rents. Then came the introduction of the Transport Supplementary Grant, the system by which local transport authorities present to the Government their proposed programmes and then are allocated funds by central government to help them carry them out. These funds are, in a sense, incorporated in the Rate Support Grant which is not allocated to specific purposes, and the money does not in theory *have* therefore to be spent on transport. Nevertheless, the reality is that central government not only determines the level of transport finance, but also has a powerful say in the ways in which it is spent. Thus the Labour Secretary of State, Mr William Rodgers, using the Conservative-introduced system, made it clear that he would effectively penalize local authorities who did not spend what he considered appropriate on support for bus services, rather than leaving it to them to decide what their needs were.

Other examples have come under the Labour government— one piece of legislation to remove a power from local government was the 1976 Education Act, which was designed to ensure that the choice of comprehensive secondary schooling was removed from local authorities. (The Labour Government of the 1960s aimed to achieve this through a circular.) Another development has been the Housing Investment Programme, by which the permitted level of council housing investment would be determined on the basis of plans submitted to the Secretary of State for the Environment, who would then decide what he was prepared to allow each local authority. This is a variant on the long-established system by which capital programmes generally have had to be approved by central government.

In addition to employing controls of this kind, government has also sought to tie local authorities more closely into central government policy in other ways. One has been the Central Consultative Council on Local Government Finance, a vehicle that is certainly not without its uses, but which also serves the equally corporatist official taste for dealing with representative associations, in this case the local authority associations. Indeed, this preference for dealing with collective bodies is one of the characteristics of modern government that needs examining closely. It is partly a matter of convenience—it is useful to be able to say that the Association of Metropolitan Authorities, or for that matter the Confederation of British Industry, the Association of Community Health Councils, or whatever, have accepted some proposal, and that therefore it is legitimized. Bureaucrat calls to bureacrat across the deep and finds an echo. Those who do not go along with such associations are left outside.

Another example of spreading corporatism may be found in the inner cities programme. The Labour Government decided that the inner city schemes should be supervised by committees made up of ministers and local authority leaders. Local authorities are seen as the main agents for action, though according to Mr Peter Shore, speaking in the House of Commons as Secretary of State for the Environment on 19 July 1977 (Hansard Vol. 935 col 1427), 'The executive function of the partnerships will be carried out by central government agencies or local government agencies'. Oddly enough, the justification for this new development was not primarily that the government was proposing to give more money, most of it through an enlarged urban programme; for the main instrument of support was to continue to be the Rate Support Grant. It was rather that the

Government was proposing to intervene more actively in the way in which RSG money was to be spent.

Behind this, of course, lay a feeling that local government had not been very effective in concentrating its efforts on the inner urban areas, and that large local authorities had not reallocated sufficient resources from their more prosperous to their more deprived areas. There were also doubts about the drive of local authorities, and about the co-ordination between local authorities and government services in matters such as employment and industry. The Partnership Committees were designed to overcome these failings. But it has to be said that the price of creating them is a reduction in local authority freedom; and that in turn raises the question of whether one can really expect local initiative to thrive if local freedom is reduced. Indeed, one wonders whether the quality of local government and the ability to get things done are not being diminished by constant government interference; demands for consultation coupled with the ever-growing web of bureaucratic processes may make decision-making and action ever harder to achieve. Like national government, local government has to do too much, and cannot do what it has to do efficiently.

Why have corporatist tendencies grown in the central-local relationship? One often-quoted reason which has some force is the desire for equality. If the government of one part of the country provides something it is felt that every other government should provide the same: there has been a constant push for more services, whether they be for consumers, the disabled, the old or other groups. The causes are normally worthwhile—though some very much more than others; but the effect is that local determination of priorities disappears under the pressure of national policies. This trend is reinforced by the impact of powerful national media, which have helped the country to think in terms of national policies and solutions rather than local policies and solutions. It is also stimulated by the growing politicization of local government, and the pressure by central party organizations on local councillors to carry out national party policy at local level—again with a loss of local freedom of action. At the same time, central government has felt bound to limit local freedom in the interests of national economic policy. This is not just a matter of the Rate Support Grant or cash limits: it is better seen through the use of central controls on capital programmes or attempts to ensure that local government conforms to national incomes policies, even when those policies are allegedly voluntary rather than statutory. Obviously when local government spends such a large proportion of the public purse, central government must be concerned with the consequences. One can hardly say that the imposition of cash limits is an unfair limitation of the amount of money to be spent on capital programmes; quite apart from the fact that so much of the cost is paid for by central government, the total level of public spending on construction is bound to concern government. The limitation on local freedom comes rather with detailed prescription of what the money may be spent on, as is done with school building programmes.

With the Rate Support Grant standing at over 60 per cent of local government expenditure, and other central government contributions on top of that, there has naturally been discussion as to whether this leads in itself to a serious loss of local freedom. One view is firmly that he who pays the piper calls the tune. The other is that the decisive factor in local freedom is the powers and duties allotted to local government, rather than the source of their finance. Thus it may be said that no one has ever shown that the local authorities which receive up to 80 per cent of their relevant expenditure in Rate Support Grant are less free than those which receive something nearer 30 per cent. The truth almost certainly lies somewhere between the two positions; but it can hardly be doubted that the trend is towards a reduction in local freedom. Could—and should—this be reversed?

I am sure it should be. Central government is far too involved in detailed decision-taking. This point was made by the Central Policy Review Staff report on 'Relations between Central Government and Local Authorities' (HMSO 1977):

The main conclusion of this report is that if central government wants to encourage corporate approaches at local level, it should, wherever possible, withdraw more in the non-interventionist direction. It should in general concentrate less on pressure and control and more on the constructive role (which it can perform far more effectively than any local authority) of promoting and issuing advice on good practice. It should as far as possible relinquish powers which it no longer needs, and pigeon-hole those it cannot relinquish. (pp. 53–54.)

This report also illustrates the gap between token commitments to decentralization and what actually happens by commenting on the system of Transport Policies and Programmes:

> Its original aim was to reduce DoE intervention in the details of local transport policies. . . . In the event the working of the TPP/TSG system has so far allowed Local Authorities a good deal less latitude than may orginally have been envisaged. The DTp feel that Councils need to be given an indicative budget or a range within which expenditure on the programme should fall, and that thereafter central government must continue to be intensively involved in the planning process. This means a virtually continuous dialogue between Counties and the DTp regional offices. . . .

In other words, a system that was designed to enhance local freedom has actually led to an increase in detailed central intervention. Not surprisingly, government has been most tempted to intervene in the politically sensitive question of support for bus services, where Labour ministers have tried to press high spending on local councils.

In the case of the Transport Supplementary Grant, the piper has had a particular power in that grants may be withheld if money is not to be spent in particular ways. Although the grant supplements the Rate Support Grant, it is specific to transport, whereas the Rate Support Grant as a whole is a general grant which can be spent broadly as the local authority wishes. Revealingly, the Labour Secretary of State for Education, Mrs Williams, has shown a desire to inject a specific element in to the grant for education.

Why do these trends matter? It is partly that government is palpably overloaded, both in Whitehall and Westminster; but beyond that, as I have suggested already, there is something deadening and depressing about the notion that local people cannot find the ability to make their own decisions, or that local authorities are not capable of making worthwhile and acceptable decisions. Of course, it is true that local elections are determined on national issues; but that owes at least something to the fact that what should be matters of local decision are in fact matters of national decision. As things stand, it is not illogical to vote for your councillors on a national party basis.

This could be reversed *if* the determination to reverse it existed and a strategy for bringing this about were worked out. Not that such a strategy could be clear-cut or proceed unimpeded to its goal: one must be realistic about the way government works, and recognize that *to some extent* local government is always liable to be used as a vehicle for national policies, and that Secretaries of State are bound to have some sort of supervisory and advisory role. It is also important to avoid the bogus—for instance the idea that health or water authorities are in some way accountable because they have a certain number of elected councillors on them, when those councillors have not been elected to deal with health or water matters and as like as not do not have any real opportunity to report back on them to the councils they represent, or to the electorate which put them on those councils. It is useful to have some councillors on these bodies, but the real accountability for both health and even the more autonomous water, under the present system, must be seen to lie with central government.

I want now to look at the structure, powers, and finance of the central/local relationship.

It must be admitted that the 1970–4 Tory Government did not get either local government or health reorganization right. True, *politically* it would have been very difficult to avoid a two-tier system—there were Labour MPs as well as Conservatives who would have fought a unitary system. Nevertheless, the duplication and blurring of responsibilities that have all too often resulted from the creation of shire counties and districts and metropolitan counties and districts are hard to justify. And that applies equally to the NHS, with its four layers of DHSS, regional health authorities, area health authorities, and districts.

The question is, what can be done about it all? Until now the predominant feeling has been that facing up to another major reorganization would be unthinkable for some time to come. I accept that: on the other hand we should start thinking about the *direction* in which we would ultimately like to see the services go, and make sure that we point any changes that do take place in that direction.

The faults of the present set-up are evident. The health service is badly over-administered at a time when resources are sadly inadequate. The 1944 White Paper on the Health Service (Cmnd 6502) said,

> There is a certain danger in making personal health the subject of a national service at all. It is the danger of over-organisation, of letting the machine designed to ensure a better service itself stifle the chances of getting one.

So too with local government. The metropolitan county councils are proving to be as gross empire-builders as the GLC was. With budgets around the £100 million mark they are overstepping their strategic role, while the fact that more than half of their budgets go on transport only shows that many of them have been pretty cavalier about their spending in that field. Worse still, there is constant friction and duplication in planning divided between the counties and the districts.

Overall, the situation in the shire counties is probably better: many of them seem to have worked out an adequate modus vivendi with the districts. Nevertheless, the confusion over planning also exists there; and the placing of education, planning, and the social services at a different level from housing breeds obvious and predictable problems.

It is tempting to say that everything should be decided at the lowest level that is compatible with overall efficiency. In some ways, that is a sound principle of administration, but it has to be qualified. If one assigns functions to different tiers on this basis, one is liable to end up with what we have at present—a proliferation of tiers. Indeed, there is pressure to create an additional regional tier. There is therefore another qualifying principle which we should pursue, and that is that real decentralized power is more likely to be achieved if it can be concentrated on as few levels as possible, indeed, preferably one really effective tier apart from central government.

This is not a simple party political battleground. Nevertheless the signs are that on the left the movement is towards a two-tier elected system based on regions and districts, with the counties eliminated. Socialists, it seems, instinctively prefer large size. They care less about the counties as traditional ingredients of the English scene; they are more impressed by academic socio-geographical planning arguments in favour of the regional units. They wish to bring the water authorities in line with the other services (a view shared by some Conservatives). In addition, they are no doubt aware that regional government would benefit them politically: a large part of the national Conservative vote would be locked up in the South-East region, thus giving Labour a better chance elsewhere.

Against this, however, are powerful alternative arguments. For a start, a regional tier would almost certainly mean much more bureaucracy—look at how the GLC and the Metropolitan counties, the nearest we have got to regions, behave. And even though in theory power might only be decentralized from London to the regions, and not moved up from the lower tier, does anyone believe that that would actually happen? Anyway, under a likely Labour plan it is pretty clear that at least part of the services like education would move from county to regional tier—so they at least would become more remote.

Moreover, there is the lack of regional affinity in many parts of the country. Eighteen million people would probably find themselves in a 'South-East' region, which would mean nothing to most of them. I doubt if belonging to the East or West Midlands means very much; and even if there is a strong regional affinity in Yorkshire, it is to Yorkshire, rather than to a North-East region in which Yorkshire might very well be placed.

My own Buckinghamshire constituents are probably typical fair number of Englishmen in their lack of regional ties. Indeed, in my own constituency we are South-East for planning, Eastern for electricity, Southern for gas, Oxford for health, Thames and Anglian for water, Wessex in the Conservative Party organization, London, Midlands and Anglia for television and Northampton for the European Parliament!

Moreover, although a regional basis may seem reasonable for some services, such as planning and water, there are others, equally important, for which the county is a very effective level of provision. Education and the social services are examples. But the real point about the county level is that it provides the opportunity of decentralizing government essentially to one strong tier, with real freedom within set limits and based on a unit which people can understand and with which they can identify themselves. No one region is perfect for all services; but the shire county comes nearest to the highest common factor.

I believe then, that our long-term aim should be to move towards unitary shire counties, which would take in all the present county and district functions. At the same time, we should move towards the area (which is the counterpart of the county) as the basis for the NHS, eliminating in due course the region above and the district below. Interestingly enough, some McKinsey consultants who advised the NHS reorganization (and I suspect then favoured a region-district pattern), have come down in favour of the same view. Apart from anything else, the district is probably too close to the actual operating unit of the hospital, which should revert to being something closer to the industrial 'profit centre', or basic managerial unit.

Naturally, there would be serious counter-arguments. The medical consultants would be reluctant to lose the regions, their present employers. Moreover, hospital services are broadly organized on a regional scale, so that the less common specialities; say neurosurgery, are provided at a regional rather than area level. But these are not insuperable difficulties, given co-operation, plus, of course, the influence of the Department of Health (which itself largely duplicates the work of the regions). Against these drawbacks there would be the great advantage of a reduction in bureaucracy; and also, of course, the possibility of a merger of health and local government under one elected body.

This would be a real prize if it could be achieved. It must certainly not be done over the dead bodies of our consultants, who have already suffered enough; and it might take a long time to persuade them that this is the right answer. But time should show that it is. This really could provide forceful decentralized government with attraction to capable people to work in it. It would also meet the major difficulty under the present pattern, that the Secretary of State is, and must be, the only accountable person or body in the National Health Service: there is no other element in it which is responsible to an electorate.

So far I have talked in terms of the shire county pattern; but the same principles should apply in the metropolitan areas.

There are arguments as to whether it should be based on present county or district level. My instinct is to say the latter, so that in effect we go back to the old county borough principle. This would require the creation of consortia of local authorities to handle police (over which the influence of local government is anyway pretty restricted), transport services, possibly the fire service, and a limited amount of strategic planning. In both shire and metropolitan areas we should make a minimum of boundary changes; the reform would essentially be to do with functions.

Does that solve the whole problem? No; there would still be some activities that should be dealt with on both broader and narrower scales than the new county level. I acknowledge that regional planning has some meaning; but the right answer is to accept, as we do now, that it is something which is bound to concern central government. We are not a very big country geographically, and the economics, planning, and transport of our various regions are inevitably interdependent. We need to make sure that where matters are in fact decided centrally this is openly acknowledged; at present central government too often pretends that some other body is responsible, and therefore it escapes proper scrutiny. It would be an important part of this approach that Parliament should be more actively concerned in such things as planning policy, which is at present very much the preserve of the executive.

Meanwhile, nearer the ground, we should accept the principle of the parish or neighbourhood council; indeed enhance it. There should be a place to which people could feel they most fully belonged, whether it be a village, a part of a town or a whole town.

Each 'place' would have its elected council, which would serve both ceremonially as the representatives of the place, and also as a forum for those who live in it. Its powers of provision might be limited, perhaps to amenities; but it would have the job of expressing the views of its citizens and of summoning its councillors on the main local authorities to hear and respond to them. Moreover, it might well take on the rather unsatisfactory role of the Community Health Councils.

This, then, is in broad terms the overall pattern we should aim at. The task now is to persuade people generally that it

makes sense, and then to move towards it with as little upheaval
as possible. Where there are disputes about functions under the
present dispensation, the functions concerned should go to the
potentially unitary tier. Both in health and local government,
existing districts might start to be merged into areas or shire
counties in anticipation of the major reform. At this stage,
however, it is discussion and persuasion that really matter; yet
the time when it makes sense to act may come sooner than most
of us have so far believed.

The right pattern of organization is a prerequisite to strengthened local government, but the actual allocation of powers as
between central and local government is also crucial.

If we look at this problem in terms of the present statutory
central-local relationship, we can see a pattern that has grown
up partly by historical accident and partly reflects the different
natures of the major services. The 1944 Butler Education Act
embodies the most subtle and perhaps the most successful
approach. It starts with the bold statement of Section 1:

> It shall be the duty of the Secretary of State to promote the edu-
> cation of the people of England and Wales and the progressive
> development of institutions devoted to that purpose, and to
> secure the effective execution by the local authorities, under his
> control and direction, of the national policy for providing a
> varied and comprehensive educational service in every area.

This statement is backed up by a number of important powers,
including substantial influence over the provision of resources,
various powers of inspection and supervision, and powers over
teachers, certain examinations, and standards or provision. The
Secretary of State has two formidable weapons in Section 68 of
the Act (the power to prevent unreasonable exercise of functions) and Section 99 (which provides default powers if local
authorities or managers or governors fail to perform their
duties)—though Section 68 grants less sweeping power since the
Courts decided in the Tameside case that the Secretary of State
himself had to behave reasonably in invoking this power. He also
has the important power under Section 13 of approving or
preventing changes in the character of schools—a power that
has been taken further by the rather cloudy conditions requiring
comprehensive secondary education of the 1976 Education Act.

The Secretary of State for Education, with certain other duties as well, looks to be a powerful being: yet the actual running of school and further education in this country is primarily a matter for the local authorities. As I put it in my short book *The Act and the Partnership* (Bedford Square Press for the Centre for Studies in Social Policy, 1976, p. 15),

> While local government is in theory the creature of central government, in that it is set up by government-drafted legislation and its powers are circumscribed and sometimes ultimately supervised by central government. it is nevertheless a creature to which its creator has given a considerable measure of free will. . . . And in contrast . . . to the NHS regions and areas, local authority duties are not in essence delegated powers.

This is an important point. In the NHS there is only one accountable entity—the Secretary of State. He delegates his powers to regions, which in turn delegate to areas, which in turn work through districts. He may hand over certain significant decisions—for instance to close hospitals—to particular tiers, but formal responsibility for the running of the service lies with him alone. Inevitably this makes for a high degree of bureaucracy—though perhaps it need not be such a high degree as we have at present!

At least both education and health are run on the basis of defined relationships; the administration of housing, by contrast, is thoroughly haphazard in its design. Indeed, it has never been set out in the way that education and health have been. The essence of the relationship has been financial, based on the system of subsidies and loan sanctions from central government. In providing these subsidies, central government has been able to attach conditions, and there are also central building regulations. Thus the Secretary of State is able to require, for example, Parker Morris standards for public-sector house-building. More recently, the Labour government has launched its system of Housing Investment Programmes, which are designed to replace the method by which local government (for a time) was able to build as many houses as it liked, safe in the knowledge that government would provide the statutory proportion of subsidy. Now, however, the plan is that local authorities should submit schemes on broadly the lines of the Transport

Policies and Programmes. These Housing Investment Programmes were described in the DoE Circular 63/77, 'Housing
Strategies and Investment Programmes: Arrangements for
1978/1979.' The scheme is

> designed to enable local authorities to present coordinated
> analyses of housing conditions in their area and to formulate
> coherent policies and programmes of capital spending on public
> housing;

and it is said that

> The strategies and programmes which Local Authorities submit
> will strongly influence the pattern of allocations and national
> priorities for housing expenditure; they will enable the Govern-
> ment to allocate resources according to comprehensive assess-
> ments of need and to plan national expenditure by reference to
> the kinds of capital expenditure which Authorities think most
> appropriate.

That may sound reasonable in principle; but the stress on the
local authority role in the sentences just quoted seems to
camouflage the fact that central government now proposes to
approve or disapprove local housing policies in a way which
has never been true in the past. No doubt there has always been
the power to grant or withhold loan sanction; but the new
Housing Strategies and Investment Programmes which have to
be submitted via DoE regional offices are fairly detailed sub-
missions, and the government will be in a position both to have
an appreciable greater impact on the pattern of local authority
housing spending and to give or withhold support from particular authorities' programmes. Once again, local freedom is being
curtailed.

The system under which the local authority personal social
services operate is broadly closer to education. Under the Local
Authority Social Services Act of 1970,

> Local Authorities shall, in the exercise of their social services
> functions, including the exercise of any discretion conferred by
> any relevant enactment, act under the general guidance of the
> Secretary of State. (Section 7i.)

The Secretary of State has a Social Work Service, which is roughly comparable to the education Inspectorate, but he has no general powers of direction. Instead, he works by guiding, sending circulars, requesting local authorities to draw up 10 year plans, disseminating information, and so on. There are other powers and duties, including those under the Chronically Sick and Disabled Persons Act of 1970; but overall it seems fair to say that the Secretary of State works through influence more than direct power. For a service which is still in many respects young, this degree of paternalism is probably not excessive.

Overall, however, the services discussed above (apart from the NHS) together with parts of transport, are essentially local authority-administered services, where the aim should be to allocate as many decisions as possible to the local bodies. Central government's control over how local authorities determine housing investment, transport, the pattern of secondary education, and so on, should be reduced; so should detailed control of building programmes. The freedom that the Labour government offered to the Scottish Assembly to work within an overall capital budget could well be offered to English major authorities.

Cash services and income maintenance, however, might well be placed still more firmly in the hands of central government than they are at present. Of course, social security is a central government service; but there is a good case for saying that the entire cost of rent rebates and allowances, school meals and milk support, uniform grants, concessionary fares, discretionary education awards, and similar benefits should fall on the taxpayer, even if in some cases the service should continue to be locally administered for convenience. The present situation encourages the proliferation of means tests as well as variations of a particularly unpalatable kind (notably in concessionary fares and discretionary awards); and it is logical to look at the pattern of incomes maintenance as a whole, so that one day we might aim to get rid of several of the means-tested or discretionary benefits and concentrate on achieving a tolerable overall level of income (presumably based on a tax credit scheme) to meet travel costs, school meals and so on.

In this case, the right basic level of provision is therefore the national one; in other cases, we need to transfer powers from local government back to the individual. Repealing the Community Land Act, with its ultimate duty for local authorities to acquire all substantial development land, is one example of this; but it is possible to envisage a more substantial shift in the field of planning than that. It is worth devoting a little space to a consideration of this argument.

The present system of development control resembles a tribal system, with a big white chief or district commissioner in the background. The members of the elected planning committee are the elders of the tribe, and they have two principal jobs. They take a general view of how their areas should develop, if at all, and they resolve disputes between members of the tribe, such as whether one man's decision to put up a dwelling will hurt that man's neighbour. In other words, they have an almost judicial role, although their right to exercise it derives not from their skill in administering the law, or their knowledge of the theory and practice of planning, but from the fact that they have been elected. In a sense, they are there to reflect the judgements of ordinary people, of their neighbours, although they are something more than simply the twelve good men and true of the jury system.

The elders have, in fact, a good deal of scope and discretion, some of it a pretty arbitrary nature. There is also the *possibility* of corruption, either by direct bribery or by the pressures of the old boy network or old pal's act. To meet these risks, therefore, there is an overlord in the form of the Secretary of State for the Environment, who can exercise both a superior judgment and superior justice. He is the District Commissioner.

This system has a number of virtues and it is argued that it has served us well. It means that planning can be reasonably democratically controlled: the power of decision at both national and local levels finally lies with accountable elected representatives. An increasing element of public participation has given those affected a chance to air their views before decision are taken. It is relatively cheap to most of those who make use of it, in that the administrative costs are borne by the public (the cost of representation at enquiries can, of course, be another matter). It provides for interaction between elected laymen and professional planning officers. It is flexible, in that planning committees can often fit their decisions to particular circumstances rather than to general rules or broad plans. And it is able, in theory anyway, through its detailed operation, to prevent monstrosities and to safeguard certain standards.

That is not a bad list, and there are many who will say that the system has given this country as good a planning system as can be found; they will point to such things as the halting of ribbon development ane the tightening of the outlines of our towns and villages as evidence of this. Some, indeed, would say that the present system should go further and abolish the basic principle recently restated by the Labour government in its DoE circular 9/76,

> that planning permission should be granted unless there is a sound and clear-cut planning reason for refusal. The onus, therefore, lies on the Authority to show that proposed development is not acceptable, rather than on the applicant to show that it is.

It is argued that the authority's approach should be neutral, or even that the onus of proof should lie with the applicant.

That, of course, would be highly controversial (and in my view undesirable); but even without that change it has to be recognized that the system as it stands is running into growing criticism on a variety of grounds.

For a start, there is the feeling that our system has not produced a truly beautiful post-war environment. It is difficult to generalize, but clearly results since 1947 have been no more than mixed. Second, it is argued that our planning system has caused needless delays and generated much red tape and that these have added heavily to the cost of building. Third, some believe that control over matters of aesthetic architectural judgment by lay elected representatives, backed by officers whose qualifications may not include architecture, is absurd. Four, there is still the risk of corruption to which I have referred; and coupled with that is the fact that the settlement of disputes between interested parties is carried out by non-judicial bodies, who may not be equipped to take an impartial view. At the same time, it can be held that the mass of detailed decision-taking that goes on in a planning department is a distraction from the proper work of *planning* a locality, and that the skills of planners are misdirected. Finally, it is argued that the present system may mean that decisions are taken on political rather than 'pure' planning grounds—that the yea or nay to a new housing estate or private hospital could depend on whether the committee liked the activity rather than on its land-use implications. (Of course, in reality it would be extremely difficult to make a sharp division between political and planning judgements.)

In my view, we should consider very carefully the possibility that detailed planning (except perhaps in conservation areas and certain other places) is not needed, and concentrate instead on the provision of local plans which—once they had been accepted —would be binding. At the same time, there would be strict regulations concerning building standards and such things as the permissible distance between the windows of two houses— the stuff of bye-laws, if you like. There would be no aesthetic control, at least where the building was designed by qualified architects. There would be a stronger law of nuisance, so that argument between neighbours about noise, loss of amenity, and so on would become a matter for the law rather than for the planners. Planning committees and staffs would then concentrate on overall planning, and the question of whether or not a development was acceptable would become a matter of whether or not it conformed with the legally-based plans and with the general law on nuisance and the environment. Objection to a proposed development would presumably be pursued through an injunction to prevent building beforehand, or through prosecution or civil action afterwards.

In effect, of course, this would mean something like the zoning and plot ratio system used in other countries, although authorities would be able to choose between a 'no-plan' system or very detailed local plans. Perhaps, too, the emphasis in planning might be on the consequences of use, rather than on the specific use itself. We should ask whether something actually creates a nuisance, or if it is simply one of a list of forbidden items.

This would mean moving away from the tribal system to a system made up of planning proper on the one hand, and legal or judicial enforcement on the other. The case for it has to do with speed, freedom, and the removal of the power of conferring or withholding favours in a somewhat arbitrary way. The case against it has to do with the risk that legislation would create inflexibility to new developments or special cases, increased cost of litigation, and with the belief that detailed development contol through elected bodies has produced an effective and acceptable system. It would be valuable if one could experiment with the different approaches side by side, but that is rarely possible in government. Perhaps all one can say is that we have had so much administrative reform that the onus of proof should lie very clearly with those who propose drastic change rather than evolutionary reform. But there is a strong case for considering it.

The planning world is not afraid of admitting that it may have made mistakes; we can see that in self-questioning about massive re-development, high rise flats, and the sharp separation of industry from housing. Is it an inevitable consequence of planning that mistakes of this kind should be made? Can planning ever be as sensitive as non-planning? I do not know, but if we are to give planning and development control a fresh direction, it should certainly be away from detailed regulation and towards greater freedom within the outline of an overall plan. Planning offers a real chance to 'de-bureaucratize'.

In planning, therefore, there is a case, not for transferring power from central to local government, but for removing detailed decisions affecting individuals from the sphere of government, so that government at any level may concentrate on those things which it can do better than anyone else. The official machine must disengage from detailed decision-making whenever it can.

In other matters, however, the need is to accept that central government is bound to make planning decisions, but to make sure that these are open and subject to effective Parliamentary procedure. I have argued already that regional plans should at the very least be examined by a Select Committee. The procedure for approving important roads also needs to be converted from a purely executive decision.

At present, when the Secretary of State wishes to create a new stretch of trunk road, he publishes a draft order setting it out. He has to state the general effect of the proposed order and he notifies those particularly affected by it. If there are objections from certain specified bodies, he has to hold an enquiry; if they come from other bodies or individuals he may do so. Following the enquiry, he may confirm, alter, or drop the scheme. If a scheme goes ahead, it is authorized by order.

The 1959 and 1971 Highways Act, which establish the procedure, also provide for the side roads needed to feed into the trunk road; again, there is provision for objection and enquiry, though in this case the final order authorizing the road is known as a Local Order, as opposed to a Line Order. Where there is an enquiry it is conducted under statutory rules.

Perhaps the crucial point to remember about the present system, however, is that the decision as to whether or not there should be a road is not a judicial decision, but a policy decision. The Inspector who conducts the enquiry is not there in the role of a judge coming to a decisive verdict. Certainly he has to conduct the enquiry according fair procedures; but his job is simply to report the objections to the Secretary of State who will decide what to do. The Inspector may, or may not, make a recommendation of his own.

Much of the hostility which the present system has aroused simply reflects the fact that some people hate roads. Changing the procedure will not assuage them. There is at least a prima facie case for saying that the Line Orders, by which trunk roads are established, should require Parliamentary approval, even though the Local Orders for side roads do not. I see this as a negative procedure—which means that the order would be automatically passed unless members (or peers) prayed against it; but at least this would mean that if there were strong opposition to the principle of the road, Parliament, rather than the Secretary of State, would decide. There would still, of course, continue to be the right to object, to hold an enquiry and so on, before the order was made.

It is true that objections (or 'prayers') under the negative procedure are not necessarily debated; but if they have significant support they should be. The realities of the Parliamentary timetable seem to make the affirmative procedure, under which Statutory Instruments *have* to be positively approved, unrealistic. At the same time, we might have to redefine which sorts of scheme would have to go before Parliament, and which would be subject only to the Secretary of State's order, as at present.

The aim of this change would be to enhance the validity of road proposals. It would also meet the difficulty of whether objectors to side roads should be able to question the validity of the major road. Under pressure, the Inspectors have moved towards allowing this to happen; but in some ways this has resulted in an illogical situation. If Parliament had made the decision, then it would be clear that the underlying strategy could not be challenged by a local enquiry concerned with one particular piece of its implementation.

The point in this instance is that decisions about the national trunk road system have to be taken at national level, and should therefore be brought under Parliamentary supervision: my argument in this case is not that the *level* of decision should be changed, but that, as a policy matter, it should be based more firmly in the political realm. And once again it has to be said that though giving a full hearing to supporters and objectors is an important part of the process, the final decision must lie with those who have been elected to take decisions about government.

Perhaps the most difficult and controversial decisions about the central/local relationship are those which concern the system of local government finance.

Although it seems unlikely that the principal recommendation of the Layfield Report on 'Local Government Finance', a local income tax, will be passed, the report nevertheless provides a valuable examination of this issue. Indeed, its main theme is the choice between increased central responsibility and increased local responsibility. In his 'Note of Reservation', Professor Alan Day argues that the committee has in effect over-polarized the issue and that a middle way can be taken, but I am sure that the committee was right to point out clearly the alternative paths.

The report makes the point that the trend has been towards centralization. It argues (p. 70) that

the Rate Support Grant determination has in the last two years become an occasion for the Government to give increasingly detailed guidance to local authorities about their pattern of expenditure. It is fair to say, however, that this development was fostered by the local authorities themselves asking for advice in situations where unpopular decisions had to be taken either to cut services or to hold back their improvement. This unwillingness is in our view a consequence of increasing reliance on grants to finance local services.

Later, on page 71, the report argues that the Consultative Council on Local Government Finance, which was set up in 1975, may also reinforce the trend:

> unless there is a clear definition of the roles of central and local government the Consultative Council may provide, among other things, another instrument for the government to use in exerting pressure on local authorities. We accept the need for closer consultation between central and local government over the planning of expenditure. . . . However, in our view, the problem will not be solved by sharing local responsibilities, even if there is agreement on aims. It is only by allocating responsibility to the parties who are to carry out those aims that continued confusion can be avoided.

This last is an absolutely vital point: the notions of partnership and joint responsibility almost inevitably lead to a further shift of power from local to central government, and to the growth of State corporatism. But Layfield's crucial argument is that 'a larger local tax base is, in our view, an essential first step to increasing local responsibility' (p. 80). This would have important consequences.

The Government's ability to influence the level of services would decline; local authorities would have to face up to more difficult decisions and be less able to shift either the decisions or the blame for them on the Government; the Government would be less able to use the financial weapon (for example, loan sanction) to achieve policy changes and would have to put them through Parliament; the annual grant negotiations would, happily, become less significant; and greater responsibility for local authorities would have to be matched by an improved audit system.

Of course the target of de-centralization faces great political difficulties. The public seems to lean towards uniformity rather than variety of provision, and egalitarians certainly do; the Treasury will be reluctant to slacken its financial control; ministers prodded by Parliament and the media are always under pressure to impose their will; and anyway, as Layfield points out, the heterogeneity of the present local government structure 'presents serious obstacles to any rationalization of the financial system, and not least to the design of financing arrangements suitable for a situation in which there would be more local responsibility'. Nevertheless, the prize of effective localism is worth pursuing.

Layfield argues (p. 246) that under it there would be two essential features for control of expenditure. The main responsibility should be with local government; and the central government's responsibility should be limited to its concern with the management of the economy, to be achieved through better mutual understanding of the problems and financial restraints and incentives which would influence the levels of total Local Authority taxation and expenditure. Any central government influence over the level of provision and expenditure on individual services should be the 'subject of separate and overt measures' rather than of financial controls like loan sanction which were not designed as ways of shaping policy.

What is needed, then, is a system by which local government raises enough of its revenue itself to feel that it can stand on its own feet, while central government retreats from its constant interference in local policy through the use of capital controls, circulars and so on and accepts that if it wants local government to pursue a particular policy it must pass a law to that effect. Thus responsibility may become more clear-cut.

This is an appealing approach; but how *is* local government to raise a greater share of its revenue? And in what circumstances should a new system be introduced?

There is no need to rehearse the difficulties which have been met over decades by those who have attempted to propound a new system of local government finance. The Conservative Party pledged itself to abolish the domestic rate in its October 1974 Manifesto; but by late in 1978 at least had still not made clear how this was to be achieved. Layfield came up with a local income tax to support the rate (recognizing the political difficulty of increasing the already unpopular rate burden); but at a time when the emphasis is on reducing direct taxation, this has won little backing. Other people have argued that the correct strategy is to switch to some form of taxation on expenditure; or alternatively simply to allow an increasing share of local government spending to be derived from general taxation—which, of course, is the reverse of the Layfield localist approach.

As one who was for a time Conservative spokesman on local government matters (and who indeed reiterated the 1974 pledge to abolish the domestic rate) I think I understand the hazards in this area. I also feel that the Layfield *objective* of greater local responsibility is right. I have suggested earlier in this chapter that it is not altogether true that he who pays the piper calls the tune in this respect: the powers conferred under the 1944 Education Act, for example, define the local authority's scope for decision more than the mechanisms of financial control do. Moreover, the rate does make it possible to distinguish between an extravagant and a cheese-paring council. Nevertheless, the fact that central government is the major provider of local government revenue can hardly fail to have influenced the growing corporatism or central influence in the central/local relationship that I have already summarized.

How do we alter this situation? The chances of eliminating a property tax in the reasonably near future look slender: the best hope of making the domestic rate more acceptable would seem to lie in the addition of some sort of supplementary householder tax, by which on top of a possibly reduced domestic rate there was a percentage supplement of, say, 20 per cent for each potential wage earner above the householder and his spouse. This would meet the basic objection to the rate, that it is unfair, but it has to be added that there are practical objections which may prove too severe, in particular the difficulty of producing sufficiently up-to-date registers of residents. A localized expenditure tax, attractive though it may be in principle, also raises practical problems discussed by Layfield.

It may then be necessary to consider a local income tax after all; but an expenditure or an income tax would only be worth implementing in the context of a reformed structure of the kind that I have discussed earlier in this chapter—that is, a basically unitary system which could take in health as well. This would provide strong enough units, with a sufficient revenue need, to make the introduction of a new system administratively worthwhile; moreover the income tax demands of the new units would be matched by corresponding reductions in the income tax contributions to central government (which would still, incidentally, be responsible for collecting the income tax on behalf of the local authorities). Finance and structure must ultimately be dealt with together, while the reform of local finance can be examined only in conjunction with our tax system as a whole.

The search for a stronger decentralized element in our system of government, with more clear-cut powers, must go on; the decentralized government should be unitary in its nature; it should as far as possible use existing boundaries and loyalties, and it should have a strong revenue base of its own. And even though, ultimately, it would still be the creature of central government, in the sense that it is its creation and subject to its laws, as well as in receipt of grant from it, nevertheless it would be firmly pegged to the notion that the way to get the best out of people is to disperse real responsibility to them. The nature of such responsibility must become sharper, rather than continually more smudged.

7

I have argued throughout this book that the locus of power in our country should be clearly defined; that where possible it should be decentralized; but that in the final analysis it should lie very clearly with Parliament, operating parallel to the courts. I have taken the view that the threat *to* Parliament is greater than the threat *from* Parliament. Nevertheless, I accept that the Commons needs some more effective counterweight than exists at present—the best being an elected, reformed second chamber. Parliament also needs to operate more competently and act as a more effective check on the executive than it often does at present.

I reject the two main varieties of corporatism—both that which permits equal bargaining between different corporations and the government, and that which sees the corporations as instruments of government; and I do not wish to see the principal corporate bodies (TUC and CBI, or variants on them) given a formal constitutional status with automatic representation in a house of Parliament. Parliament must represent individuals, not collectivities, and it is a simple matter of principle that management and unions should not be given what is in effect an additional vote.

But again, I do not want to see Parliament or Whitehall running everything. I want a truly effective, strong unitary system of *local* government, which would cover health care, and would certainly not be a mere agent of central government. Nor should political parties (through state subventions), business, professions, families, or individuals become ever more dependent on government.

Such, in brief, is the message of this book—which was written, and sent to the printer, before the avalanche of strikes that began

with the Ford and road haulage disputes at the end of 1978 and
continued in the new year with the prolonged outburst of public
sector militancy. As I write this postscript, what Mr Callaghan
likes to call the 'spasm' is not over; but enough has happened to
force me to ask whether it has invalidated what I have written
and whether there are any conclusions that can be drawn or
redrawn about the problem of power in our society.

The period of the 'spasm'—or 'chasm' as it has seemed to
many—raised the question of the power of parliamentary government in a more acute form even than it had been raised in the
winter of 1973–74. For a while, through the medium of the press
and television, government by picket or strike committee has
seemed to be the order of the day, and there has been deep resent-
ment at the way in which ministers and others have had to go to
unions to ask for concessions. Immediate judgements while a
crisis is under way may not always be the wisest, but inevitably
the question of new legislation has been revived. At the very
least the law over picketing, especially secondary picketing,
seems bound to be reviewed and the search intensified for some
way of settling disputes about pay in life and death services like
hospitals, ambulances and the fire service without industrial
action. The closed shop is back on the agenda. Perhaps most
fundamental of all, the argument is being revived that we shall
never achieve satisfactory industrial relations until agreements
can be made binding.

But what did the outburst tell us—if only tentatively—about
the relationship between union, governmental and parliamentary
power?

As far as the unions were concerned, the events were a
reminder of what the Donovan commission on unions and
employers' associations had argued ten years before—that power
is moving towards the shopfloor. The Ford strike which triggered off the whole sequence was certainly marked by an in-
stantaneous rank-and-file rejection of the government's pay
norm—a rejection the ferocity of which took both management
and union leaders by surprise. The same mood was to be found
among the road haulage men, and it was repeated at times in the
public sector disputes—though it appears that in at least one of
the major public sector unions, NUPE, the leadership *was*
militant. It was keen to show the union's industrial muscle,

hoping in the process not only to demonstrate that public sector workers could not be taken for granted but also to build up its own membership.

The demonstration of shopfloor power and independence has significant implications for the locus of power in our country. On the one hand, it makes it harder for government to use the unions as an instrument for implementing its policy—Mussolini-type corporatism, tripartitism and a social contract will all be that much harder to bring about if power really is moving to the shopfloor. On the other hand, it did not prevent the Labour government from trying to revive the social contract approach—and indeed partially succeeding *if* the so-called 'concordat' or joint statement by the TUC and the Government (in that order on the cover of the white paper!) proves to have any more than a very transient significance. All that can be said at this stage is that the TUC leaders rallied round to try to keep Labour in power (or anyway in government); but it seems doubtful whether the shopfloor genie can so easily be put back in the bottle.

Indeed, opponents of state corporatism may take some heart from the apparent trend. For while a decentralisation of union power produces obvious difficulties for government and un-certainties in the mechanisms by which society controls itself, it may also restore some of that flexibility and responsiveness to particular local and economic circumstances which more mono-lithic arrangements make difficult to achieve. This particularly applies to national-scale pay policies and bargaining, which are inevitably insensitive.

But of course it is harder to get away from national-scale approaches in the public than in the private sector. I said earlier in this book that the unions may be reaching the apogee of their power, and I believe that to be true in the private sector. I also believe that the private sector—left to itself—could have coped reasonably effectively with the strikes of this past winter. Both Ford and the road hauliers could probably have reached a quicker and less expensive settlement without government guidelines. Incomes policies, whether voluntary or statutory, may provoke conflict where none would otherwise exist.

But the public sector is a different matter, and we may have to face the possibility of continued increased militancy in it. After all, the best answer to militant or over-defensive unions in the private sector is to show that the way to greater prosperity is through higher productivity and greater efficiency. The evidence is there that new technology and improved output have not meant greater overall unemployment. But in the public services the concept that creating more wealth means potentially more money for all does not so obviously apply: the temptation to fight aggressively for more will be all the greater. Moreover, almost intuitively the unions have come to realise that if they want to hurt their 'bosses' by industrial action, that means hurting the public as a whole, who are their bosses.

How is government to respond to this new tendency? Inevitably, there must be two sides to the response: one, as a humane and sensible employer, but the second as the guardian of the public interest.

As to the first, this entails making sure that the pay and conditions of those who work in the public sector are reasonable and not out of line (allowing for index-linked pensions and job security) with those in the private sector. It entails avoiding the sort of social and economic nonsense that has led lower paid public sector workers to have to rely on means-tested benefits to supplement their incomes so that even when their pay has been increased they have been left in the poverty trap. The vital need here is to take lower paid workers out of direct taxation as soon as possible.

But at the same time, there must be some sort of discipline in upholding the public interest, and both central and local government must be prepared to check the power of the public sector unions where it becomes excessive. This is partly a matter of economic instruments such as cash limits and the realisation that excessive pay must lead to fewer job and reduced services. It is also a matter of an absolute insistence that where vital services are threatened, the government will always maintain them by some means or other. Government must also insist on the principle that the right to strike does not extend to the right to pick and choose which parts of your job you do and still expect to be paid in full—something that has happened all to often recently.

In other words, in its own sector the government must be willing to manage, and the weak leadership, or lack of leadership, which has marked the Department of Health for example, cannot go on. But good management must not be seen in purely negative terms. There is a job to be done in improving industrial relations in the National Health Service, and that job includes finding a way of establishing reasonable levels of pay so that the right to take industrial action where health is concerned may be renounced. The same applies in the other life and death services. No-strike agreements will be hard to achieve because union leaders hate to shed their own weapons; but in fact experience over the past decade shows that agreements embodying the indexing of pay would have been greatly to the benefit of many public sector employees.

There is a major task for government in reasserting its authority in the public sector, but what about Parliament? How has it come out of the 'spasm'?

In some ways, it has performed its traditional role effectively. It has certainly subjected ministers to intensive scrutiny and voiced effectively the deep public concern about what was happening. It also seems fair to say that it secured some improvement in the situation. Ministers were thrown on the defensive and in turn had to use such influence as they had on the unions to try to persuade them to moderate the way in which the disputes were conducted. This led to the concordat which at least showed that the Labour movement saw that there had been serious abuses which had to be put right. It is something to have that document on the record.

But against this it must be said once again that the concordat represented a private deal between the unions and government with Parliament having no say in the matter. It must also be said that in two vital respects Parliament does not do its job as it should.

The first is that Parliament has not provided the continuous informed and searching analysis of these admittedly difficult problems that have led us to the present situation. The quality of its analysis of our economic and industrial policies has been inadequate, and insofar as such analysis has taken place the results have not been driven home effectively. It is for this sort of reason that we have to change the procedures of the house, both in the committee system and on the floor. The problem of how to feed in the findings of a strengthened committee network into the Chamber looks all the more pressing.

Secondly, Parliament must be regarded not only as an arena for conflict but also as a place where agreement and consensus may sometimes be sought. The conflict is important. The parties stand for principles more fundamental than the simple pursuit of power. Moreover, attack—as I have just suggested with regard to recent events—is a part of the process of pressing government to take what seem to be the right decisions. Equally, the adversarial process, as our courts testify, is often an effective method of arriving at the truth, or at least an acceptable solution.

Nevertheless, agreement is also necessary in a civilised society, and Parliament should be a place where agreement is sought if possible. As I have said already, the initiatiative in seeking agreement must lie predominantly with government, but other parties have their part in it. I certainly hope that when we come to power we shall use Parliament where we can as an instrument through which to reconcile, rather than to dominate.

Index

117